A Story Of Invisible Power
A Path Towards Jiu Jitsu Principles & Execution

By

Tony Pacenski
M.A. Edu.

To. TSgt Wise,

Thank you for all the energy
and instructions during our ISD
ALS class.

Best
Pat. "Little"
Tony

Copyright © 2015 Written by Tony Pacenski

Photography by Matt Hurchick

Cover by Patricia Pacenski

All Rights Reserved.

ISBN- 13:978-1541197053

ISBN – 10:1541197054

Second Edition English

A Story Of Invisible Power
A Path Towards Jiu Jitsu Principles & Execution

DEDICATION

I dedicate this book to the great masters of Jiu
Jitsu from Brazil that trained, developed the art
through education and blood on their hands
from combat in the field or in the arena. Their
life's commitment to Jiu Jitsu has given
practitioners a life philosophy and self-defense
system for personal development.

WARNING AND DISCLAIMER

The information and techniques in this book, when used properly, can provide you with the means to protect yourself and your loved ones from attackers. Be aware that the techniques continued herein could cause serious injury and even death. You are solely responsible for any and all use or misuse of these techniques. Please use the utmost caution when studying and practicing this material.

The author, demonstrators, photographers, distributors and any others involved with this book are in no way responsible for the use or misuse of the material contained in this book.

The content of this book is solely the opinion of the author and is based on his many years of training in the area of practical self-defense. The author has researched all the techniques demonstrated and presents the results to you in this book. The teaching in this book is for informational purposes only. Please train only with a qualified instructor.

Please consult a certified instructor before training in any martial art or engaging in any physical activity.

iii

ACKNOWLEDGEMENTS

"Before the arrow(s) is shot, it is important to believe you will hit the mark. In holding the bow, it is important to thank those that believe in you and trust you will hit the mark! The release is a single breath."- Prof. Tony Pacenski – California, 2013

I would like to thank Rickson Gracie for all of your trust and belief in me to help in the formation of the Jiu Jitsu Global Federation. Along the way I was so grateful to find a brother and new family. You have inspired and enlightened so many generations of Jiu Jitsu practitioners, fighters and instructors.

Para meu irmão Carlos Gama, obrigado por todas as longas horas e orientação. Tenho aprendido muito com os seus exemplos e ideias. Tamojunto. All the best to you and your family Capitão always!

I want to thank my mentor and friend "The Pitbull" Leonard Rosen for all of the lessons about business and life.

I want to thank my mom for always believing in me and supporting each big action I take in my life. I want to thank my father for all the examples of being a man, his work ethic and to show me to go after what I want because life is a whisper.

I want to thank Steve Maxwell my 1st Gracie Jiu. Jitsu instructor for being a pioneer on the east coast of the United States and bringing Gracie family Jiu Jitsu to all of us in Philadelphia, Pennsylvania.

I want to thank my friend Matt Hurchick for all of his video work and photographs over the years. Yet more importantly, I want to thank him for his friendship all these years and his sense of humor. I want to thank my family the Saffaies in California for their love & support and Claudia Gadelha for your daily reminders to grind, trust and for of course saving me in Brazil. Also to Camila Xavier for showing me my heart is strong and for giving me the motivation to write this book.

I want to thank my teammates on the Jiu Jitsu teams I've been a part of including the different Gracie Jiu Jitsu teams: The Gracie Academy, Relson Gracie Team, Maxercise, Elite, Carlson Gracie South Bay and BJJ Revolution Team with Prof. Rodrigo Medeiros (my master) and Master Julio "Foca" Fernandez for the blessing to chase my dreams. Also, a special thanks to Soke Michael DePasquale for your life's work in Jiu Jitsu & being an original motivation to me to learn about Jiu Jitsu before the Gracie Family. Lastly, I want to thank Rose Gracie for all of her years of support and friendship. You're the toughest Gracie I ever met!

v

ABOUT THE AUTHOR

Anthony "Tony" J Pacenski Jr. helped co-found the Jiu Jitsu Global Federation (JJGF). He has been taught by many of the top Jiu Jitsu instructors in the United States and Brazil since 1995. Tony has worked as a Jiu Jitsu instructor since 1996 and spent two years in the Gracie Jiu Jitsu instructor program in Torrance, California. Tony has worked with a diverse group of students including Military and Law Enforcement, children, women's self-defense, and general practitioners. Having received instruction from Grandmaster Helio Gracie and his sons over a twenty year period, today Tony is a 3rd degree black belt professor under Rodrigo Mederios from the Carlson Gracie Team and BJJ Revolution Team. He also holds shodan level (1st degree) black belt in Yoshitsune Combat Ju-Jitsu under Soke Michael DePasquale Jr for Jiu Jitsu from Japan.

Tony has started two academies under the BJJ Revolution Team Flag: The Revolution Academy in Pennsylvania in 2004; and, the BJJ Revolution Team- Redondo Beach Academy in 2008. He is known for his passion for Jiu Jitsu and for his detailed and well-organized instruction, which are showcased in his instructional videos, industry writings, Podcasts and in his international seminars.

Tony has also been a pivotal influence in the Jiu Jitsu world by consulting martial arts academy owners in business. He holds a Master's Degree in Education in curriculum & instruction from Concordia University of Southern California Irvine. Tony is currently enlisted in the United States Air Force and is pursuing a degree in Aviation Maintenance Technology.

CONTENTS

Introduction

The first time I saw Jiu Jitsu in action was the Ultimate Fighting Championship 1 watching Royce Gracie win the tournament in 1993. By that time I was training in Tae Kwon Do and did wrestling camps in the summer. I had a monthly subscription to Inside Kung Fu Magazine because the Martial Arts I really wanted to train in were Wing Chun and Bruce Lee's philosophy of Jeet Kune Do. I was 14 years old and still wanted to be like Lee; however, by the time I was 15 years old, I lied about my age at the local restaurant to get the 16-year old busboy position.

With the money I made and the 1994 issue of Full Contact magazine with Rickson Gracie on the cover in my hands, I asked my mom to order me the Gracie Jiu Jitsu Instructional Basic Tapes made by Rorion Gracie and Royce Gracie. The articles in the Full Contact magazine talked about all the grappling systems in America at the time. The stories about Rickson Gracie and the Machado Brothers inspired me. I remember pulling out from under the sofa an atlas. I opened the book to try to find Torrance and Redondo Beach, California because these places were where Rickson and the Machado Brothers lived and trained. I can still remember my finger on the page touching Redondo Beach and thinking I am going to go there. Since I was now on the Gracie Jiu Jitsu Academy's mailing list by owning the tapes and practicing with my friends, it was no coincidence that almost one year later I found out about Steve Maxwell in Philadelphia.

One train ride later to the big city and the academy called Maxercise Sports and Fitness just a block away from the Liberty Bell, I knew Gracie Jiu Jitsu was what I wanted to do forever. At 16 I would begin formal lessons.

***

There are many things a person can learn in ten years of doing one thing. After 20 years of doing those many things learned, we realize what is most important is to do less with all the things we learned. Nonetheless, before I write the next sentence about some of the things I learned in 20 years of Jiu Jitsu, I want to thank the Gracie Family and Machado Brothers for helping to inspire my generation and so many others. Jiu Jitsu throughout your life's work has been proven to be effective and the Martial Art global community; more importantly, the world needed your Jiu Jitsu!

This book will focus on the principles and theories of Jiu Jitsu from Brazil. Gracie family Jiu Jitsu or as it is called in the United States "Brazilian Jiu Jitsu" is a grappling oriented Martial Art style with proficiency on ground fighting. Since the beginning, Brazilian Jiu Jitsu was developed out of real fighting situations standing up or on the ground. In that regard the style was based on what is real instead of what could be real. Training and learning underlined this philosophy so techniques were not designed only for sports with rules, but instead techniques were designed to effectively address the actual tactics and strategies of a real fight using practical movements instead of flashy and theatrical nonsense. Brazilian Jiu Jitsu prefers to bring an opponent to the ground and rely on grappling techniques to subdue the opponent using holds, armlocks, chokes, leglocks, and strikes. This strategy takes away the advantage of an opponent with superior striking abilities. It can also mitigate the advantage of a stronger and much larger opponent to rely on wrestling or grappling.

Benefits of Jiu Jitsu from Brazil

For all Practitioners:
Jiu Jitsu from Brazil offers a system of simple self-defense techniques that work whether you are big and strong or of a small frame. The principles of leverage on which Jiu Jitsu is founded allow a practitioner to pursue the art throughout his or her lifetime. Jiu Jitsu is also beneficial in helping maintain cardiovascular fitness. Likewise, Jiu Jitsu has been compared to a human form of chess because of the fun, endless strategies of technique and counter-technique via: armlocks, escapes, and chokeholds during class or in tournaments. Training helps the development of different ways of thinking for the practitioner. Students are taught the importance of relaxation, balance, self-control and patience that is used in Jiu Jitsu as well as in life.

For Law Enforcement & Armed Forces:
Jiu Jitsu from Brazil has proven extremely effective in Law Enforcement and the Armed Forces. The element of control emphasized in Jiu Jitsu provides the edge an officer or solder would need to subdue and arrest a suspect. While most martial arts emphasize striking, Jiu Jitsu offers a more appropriate alternative for law enforcement and the Military. Police department studies have concluded that more than 90% of confrontations in the field end up on the ground. In this scenario Jiu Jitsu allows an officer to be comfortable and in control of a situation. Jiu

Jitsu also known as "combat wrestling" has become the prototypical system for training in most police academies and Military branches around the world.

Jiu Jitsu From Brazil As A Compliment To Other Martial Arts Systems

Two goals for almost every martial artist are to be as well rounded and prepared as possible when confronted with a self-defense situation. Jiu Jitsu was confined to Brazil for nearly a century. With the introduction of the Ultimate Fighting Championship (UFC) in 1993, an awakening occurred in the martial arts community. Before the UFC, most individuals' frame of reference for martial arts came from movies and television. With the introduction of the UFC (in its original format, with no time limits or rules) everyone was able to see martial arts presented in a realistic context for the first time in America. The success of Jiu Jitsu in the UFC convinced many practitioners of other martial arts that by understanding Jiu Jitsu they would be better fighters and martial artists. Today to compete in the UFC all fighters must have an understanding and training in the Martial Art of Jiu Jitsu. This was a major objective reached of the Gracie family.

The Different Aspects of Jiu Jitsu from Brazil

There are 3 different aspects of training Jiu Jitsu from Brazil: Self-Defense training, Street-Defense training, and Sport-Tournament training.

Self-Defense Training-
This type of training involves the ability to handle standup aggression and defend oneself from a physical attack on the ground or from a weapon such as a knife, gun or club. Jiu Jitsu's self-defense addresses the most realistic attacks that occur on the street. Students are taught how to control the situation before the attack happens. Yet, if an attack comes, Jiu Jitsu will allow the student to use simple escapes and attacks geared toward controlling and finishing an assailant with submission holds. Since the holds are based on leverage, the student has the ability to use as much pressure he or she wishes to implement. In self-defense and in matters of the law it is not always the best option to strike back because you cannot punch someone soft. Jiu Jitsu gives many options to deal with an attack without striking; however, the system does teach striking from superior positions.

Street-Defense Training-

Since Jiu Jitsu was developed to reflect real

fighting on the streets of Rio de Janeiro, Brazil, this aspect of training teaches how to defend oneself, for lack of better words, in a street fight. In Brazil the word "vale tudo," which means **anything goes**, is the concept that structures class training. A student that enters a vale tudo class will learn how to take a person with superior striking abilities down to the ground, control the person, and finish the fight by submission, striking, or by verbal command. Jiu Jitsu has changed the way martial artists train because of this form of training. It is understood that one can't have a safe class lesson with people punching and kicking each other so in this class you will get very close to fighting by focusing on the little details of street fighting positions without hurting one another. In doing this, the student will learn what is real and practical instead of what could be real and is pure fantasy.

Sport-Tournament Training with or without the Kimono-

In this aspect of training students learn the many Sport Jiu Jitsu techniques and strategies. Students train with the uniform (Gi or Kimono) on and learn takedowns, throws, ground-positions, escapes, attacks and endless strategies. This is a fun way to explore Jiu Jitsu for the students that aren't interested in fighting. Also, all the techniques can be used in Jiu Jitsu tournaments that have safe rules and weight classes for children, women, and men. Another aspect focused on is training without the uniform. Students are taught Jiu Jitsu without relying on the uniform for control. This way of training is similar to wrestling, but instead of trying to pin the person as in wrestling, training is geared toward finishing the opponent with submission holds.

Jiu Jitsu Self-Defense Standing: Naked Techniques and Dressing Up Techniques | A Look At Japanese Style Strike Based Verses Brazilian Style of Grappling Based Approaches.

Firstly, it is important to look at Jiu Jitsu self-defense and handling standup aggression. If one observes 20 Brazilian Jiu Jitsu self-defense techniques to handle and address common attacks and holds by an attacker, one will quickly see that the "Brazilians" answer problems with grappling without strikes during the moves. This is not to say that the Brazilian Jiu Jitsu stylists do not use punches and kicks for self-defense or in the real fight however. The common 2 handed-choke escape is completed with a throw and armlock finish or a simple head and body escape. In both moves, there was not one strike that was applied to begin the move or during it because the details and elements are (were) pure grappling. This means the escape can be completed with ones eyes closed- Grappling is feel. Without using a strike to soften up the attacker or to make temporary pain as the detraction to transition to the core technique it is said the move was a naked technique. Adding the strikes is to dress-it -up.

In comparison, the Japanese ju jitsu stylist often in many of the different styles of Ju Jitsu from Japan will use striking techniques to dress-up the move using key strikes techniques. This is called Atemi. The common two-handed choke by an attacker will see the Japanese ju jitsu student trap of the wrist and at the same time use a strike to the face or ribs. Next, the ju jitsu stylist will transition to a locking technique, escape or throw.

It has always been interesting to me when training with different Jiu Jitsu teachers how the same attacks are defended in a self-defense situation. Recently, we used a two-handed lapel grab to see how Brazilian Jiu Jitsu answered the problem and how the Japanese ju jitsu answered the problem. In the dojo there were four of us. I was the Brazilian Jiu Jitsu representative and the three others were from the Yoshitsune Waza Ju-Jitsu system. The first two instructors addressed the problem with strikes first and then using a joint lock or throw. I added a technique to the session by using pure grappling to break the hold and finish with an elbow strike. Yes, the Brazilian Jiu Jitsu stylists do use striking and typically this is done at the end of the technique.

The last instructor used pure grappling for a quick takedown and armlock finish to address the two-handed lapel grab. I made the comment that I really liked it because it was naked the whole time with no strikes. I said that the Brazilian Jiu Jitsu community would out of the 3 techniques that I saw tonight like this last one because it did not relay on strikes before, during or after the overall technique. Furthermore, the Japanese jujitsu instructors listened to some of the ideas I was speaking about such as using grappling, clinching an attacker, taking the fight to the ground and sometimes totally disengaging were very eye raising to them. Their comments were in line with the idea of, "If you disengage from the attack, the opponent is still in front of you and can attack again. Isn't it better to do a lot of damage to end the threat?" My comments next showcased the philosophical ideas and concepts from the Gracie Family Jiu Jitsu System. I said:

> Many times when performing an isolated self-defense technique it can be flawed. It is important to have the next specific self-defense technique or tool to follow up with his. However, it is common that techniques and tools will not work. In those moments it is important to have a discipline to fall back on. If I were to be trained as a boxer, my punches, clinching and movement would help me in such a critical moment. Since my core training is in Jiu Jitsu from Brazil, I can start out with a double lapel attack and start an escape based on leverage, base (balance) and simplicity; however, if the attacker during the movement puts me in a headlock, I can do the next technique to escape. But what is important is that during the stress if the headlock escape does not work as plan, I know I am safe, knowledgeable and

comfortable in the clinch. And I am even more at home on the ground because I have spent 20 years learning how to do Jiu Jitsu this way. If I am safe in the clinch and on the ground, you must understand that distance and disengagement where the person cannot touch me is a place of safety. We need to know effectly how to manage distance. When an attacker grabs a hold of you, we really do not know what he is going to do next. Since we are being held in a grappling situation, we can train and learn to be knowledgeable and feel next what the person is going to do. And with the feel and the connection, the Jiu Jitsu will help us escape or finish the situation with or without striking.

After my speech, one of the instructors started to question the group about the idea of a bad person approaching you and taking your space. "What are you to do: punch the person first," he said? "If we did this, the cops would have a problem with us for hitting the guy first," he went on. The question went to me, "Professor Tony what would you do if the person approaches you?" I went ahead and stopped the attack by putting my hands in the attacker's body near both arms. From there, I said, "Look, I am not intimated. I did not step back and I did not throw a punch. I do not know what the person is going to do next; however, I have some great ideas of where he could go and do." I smiled and said, "Do something." The Japanese Jujitsu instructor went for the punch and I clinched. We stopped from there as my points were being made. I showed that from the hands on the chest I could close my eyes and stop what ever comes next. His arm goes high, go to the back clinch. The punch to the head, go to the front clinch and the tackle against me, not a chance. I concluded with the training concept of reoccurrence to find the timing and better personal technique in whatever we are doing in the Japanese approach or the Brazilian approach to problem solving for self-defense and training in the art of Jiu Jitsu.

*****

Reoccurrence in your training within the academy or dojo is a number one factor for real progress when learning new techniques and strategies. Being able to put yourself in the same position over and over again is going to give you the reps needed to develop practical skill. As the saying goes, "The mother of all skill is repetition!" When you continue to have the correct reoccurrence on the mat, you will deeply understand the finer points of the hook sweep for example by fully developing transitions, movements and applications of the variations to turn the fight in your favor!

One problem I see all the time in the academy or the dojo is the lack of constant training by students. A training problem occurs during the learning process very early on by the instructor and the student. Even experienced Brazilian Jiu Jitsu students will fall into the trap. This trap is practicing a move on one day and not returning to this practice for another week. Every training session matters! You find this out when you get an injury and can't roll for weeks on end! It is the students responsibly to come to the gym with a plan of positions to work on. There must be recurrence in your training or the movements will not become second nature. The hook sweep has to just happen because experienced players will break your position down and pass your guard if you are not sharp.

Don't become bored as an experienced fighter when your instructor is showing the same self-defense technique or position. Even if you are shaking your head like because you saw a basic position before during class, this is your opportunity to explore variations of technique, develop transitional movements and have reoccurrence to develop your timing, application and overall sensitivity.

Call it Jiu Jitsu

When I was a little kid, I wanted to learn Jiu Jitsu because of the desire to learn how to throw a person to the ground. I also enjoyed seeing the submission holds and pinning techniques; it reminded me of Professional Wrestling on television. Without formal instruction, I knew that Jiu Jitsu and judo were similar yet different, and much different than karate which was about punching and kicking techniques. In the Martial Arts magazines there were articles and pictures about Jiu Jitsu from Japan with self-defense techniques against punches, tackles, kicks and weapons. The classic sequences were about counter attacks while standing and taking the attacker to the ground ending in a submission hold, strike or pin. These photos were such interesting transitions and all of this was Jiu Jitsu from Japan to me.

As a teenager, I was exposed to Jiu Jitsu from Brazil seeing Royce Gracie in the Ultimate Fighting Championship & by reading the magazines about the Gracie family and their cousins the Machado brothers. Both families were cousins. I still have these magazines with interviews about Royce Gracie in 1993 and Rickson in 1994. The Gracie family had and *continue*s to have a tremendous impact in the martial arts industry. By changing the training methodologies in the schools that heavily favored kata/preset forms; connecting the important strategies, techniques and refinements of grappling and ground fighting to other aspects of standup punching and kicking; and, helping to finally have the confidence for better or worse to say "We are black belts in Jiu Jitsu, it works in a real fight and we will prove it! The Jiu Jitsu from Brazil or Gracie family Jiu Jitsu made a black belt legit through the byproducts of the Gracie Challenge against all styles of fighting! The Gracie Challenge was originally started in Brazil around 1930 all the way to the United States in the 1990's. The idea was simple: Gracie Jiu Jitsu is better than your Martial Arts style and we will test that theory now.

Today some 20 years later with experience in all types of Martial Arts training from many different countries and a 3rd degree black belt in Jiu Jitsu from Brazil, I am often asked the question what is the difference between Japanese Jiu Jitsu and Brazilian Jiu Jitsu? Before, the question people used to ask me was what is the difference between Karate and Jiu Jitsu? My answer to that question was, "Jiu Jitsu starts where karate ends." However, the question now is about Japanese Jiu Jitsu and Brazilian Jiu Jitsu.

Answering this question above is to understand a little history of Jiu Jitsu as it traveled from

Japan to Brazil and from Brazil to the United States & around the world in that order. Next is to understand curriculum differences between Jiu Jitsu in the dojo (Japan) verses Jiu Jitsu in the academy (Brazil). Finally, a little experience in knowing that when you are in Brazil you say, "I train Jiu Jitsu not Brazilian Jiu Jitsu," this will all help you understand the answer. So...1...2...3:

1: Ju-Jitsu in Japan by 1900 was a dying art form because the fall of the samurai class. Instructors of ju jitsu were known to take on other professions to make a living. In Japanese cities, the jujitsu students received bad press for fighting. It was not until a man named Kano Jigoro started his own organized system of ju jitsu originally called Kano Jiu Jitsu and would later be known as Judo, which helped Jiu Jitsu live to this day. Kano developed a belt system to allow experts to in Jiu Jitsu train with beginners and he developed a safe curriculum to not allow techniques for example such as eye poking, biting, joint breaks etc. Out of these curriculum developments and changes students could practice techniques and strategies in real time instead of katas/forms, which were preset movements without resistance. The new training method of free sparring quickly gave feedback to what worked and also at the same time gave students the ability to evolve their practice. This was known as **randori**.

Jiu Jitsu in Brazil arrived by a prize-fighter, Judo and Ju Jitsu black belt named Mitsuyo Maeda. He had traveled through Europe and the Americas

18

taking on challenge fights using his skills of Judo, Jiu Jitsu and ground fighting techniques. By the time Maeda taught Carlos Gracie the techniques of Jiu Jitsu from Japan, he was very much experienced in using his insights into combat furthering the strategies of closing the distance between his opponent in a real fight and taking the fight to the ground. Within a period of 4 to 7 years, as it was never really clear to me, Carlos Gracie would open the first Gracie Jiu Jitsu academy. Carlos taught his four other brothers the techniques learned from Maeda and, as history has proved, his younger brother Helio helped to further specific teaching methods, curriculum and refinements for Jiu Jitsu to include better leverage for techniques, performance and strategy for fighting in matches called Vale Tudo (Anything Goes) against other styles of Martial Arts. This was the birth of the Gracie Challenge to test the Gracie Family Jiu Jitsu.

During the 1980's, Rorion Gracie (Helio's oldest son) was given the credit for bringing Gracie Family Jiu Jitsu to the United States (1978). With the continued success of teaching methodologies learned from Helio Gracie and further success of the Gracie Challenge, Rorion co-founded the Ultimate Fighting Championship (UFC). As Rorion's little brother Royce Gracie armlocked and choke his way to victories in the UFC 1, 2 and 4, the style of Jiu Jitsu called Gracie Jiu Jitsu or Brazilian Jiu Jitsu was coined in the United States and around the world.

2: Jiu Jitsu can trace its roots back to the times of the samurai and the warrior class of Japan. I have always been taught the Jiu Jitsu techniques were used if the samurai was without his sword/weapon(s). Among the many techniques and strategies the samurai practiced were different types of weaponry arts and without weapons using striking tactics, grappling holds, releases from holds, joint-locks, chokeholds, throws and ground fighting. During this time frame, the samurai clans and families started many styles of Jiu Jitsu. I have read that families and clans developed hundreds of systems and schools-of-thought for Jiu Jitsu: often combining styles to create other styles of Jiu Jitsu.

Jiu Jitsu from Japan as practiced in the dojo to this day in the United States can be called Traditional Ju Jitsu. Techniques and curriculum involve release escapes and self-defense kata/forms against weapons such as the traditional sword, strikes, joint-locks and pinning verses Jiu-Jisu from Brazil as practiced in the academy in the United States and around the world outside of Brazil having a different belt ranking system, curriculum techniques and better refinements to ground fighting for competition sport and self-defense for self-preservation. This style of Jiu Jitsu is often referred to as Brazilian Jiu Jitsu or Gracie Jiu Jitsu.

3: Finally, when you have some experience in learning Jiu Jitsu and practicing it, you will over time just call it Jiu Jitsu. When you travel to

Brazil, you will say, "I train Jiu Jitsu!" When you are asked about your rank, you will say, "I am a black belt in Jiu Jitsu!" The Brazilian fighters in Brazil do not say they train in Brazilian Jiu Jitsu. They say, "I train Jiu Jitsu at this academy (academia)!" When Jiu Jitsu arrived in the United States, **Rorion Gracie** trademarked the triangle logo and text: Gracie Jiu-Jitsu. Other instructors that arrived in the United States without the last name of Gracie needed to use their own names for example Machado Jiu Jitsu. Thus, if you did not have a last name that would market well in the Martial Arts community, the term Brazilian Jiu Jitsu (BJJ) was used to express that you taught or trained in Gracie Family Jiu Jitsu in the United States and around the world.

I remember when I was in the instructor's program under Rorion, Royce and Helio Gracie being asked the question, *"What is the difference between Gracie Jiu Jitsu and Brazilian Jiu Jitsu?"* My response was that the techniques of Gracie Jiu Jitsu and Brazilian Jiu Jitsu are the same armlocks, chokes and movements; however, Gracie Jiu Jitsu is a specific teaching method developed by Grand Master Helio Gracie and showcased at the Gracie Jiu Jitsu in Torrance, California at the time.

Some questions I ask you now are about Japanese Ju-Jitsu and Brazilian Jiu Jitsu. Is Ju-Jitsu from Japan Traditional? Is the Jiu Jitsu from Brazil Modern or contemporary? Before you answer, with the continued philosophies of BJJ evolving: There is currently a movement of

Traditional BJJ verses Modern BJJ. The debate between what is old-school verses new school will always be there in the Jiu Jitsu communities in all countries. I hope all of you reading this will understand what it means to just call it Jiu Jitsu. Spell it like you want and call it what you want! Just keep practicing the art form, enjoy the sport and share your Jiu Jitsu experiences with the next generation because it is your responsibility to do just that!

Defining Gracie Jiu-Jitsu Verses Brazilian Jiu Jitsu Deeper

What is the difference between Gracie Jiu-Jitsu versus Brazilian Jiu-Jitsu? The Armlocks, Chokes and moves of Brazilian Jiu Jitsu (BJJ) are the same as Gracie Jiu-Jitsu. The difference is the teaching method. Here at the Gracie Jiu Jitsu Academy in Torrance, California we strictly endorse the teaching methods of Grand Master Helio Gracie. He believes that there is no such thing as a good or bad student: only good teachers and bad teachers.

Above was the question and answer sequence I was told to memorize, drill and say during introduction lessons at the Gracie Jiu-Jitsu Academy's instructors training program from 1998 to 2000. Today this explanation still holds truth and value. Gracie Jiu-Jitsu as we were educated to explain was a teaching methodology and not a style of jiu-jitsu; however, it was a style of Jiu-Jitsu different than the Japanese parent styles. In other words, in Brazil, Gracie Jiu-Jitsu was called Jiu-Jitsu. In the United States it was called Gracie Family Jiu-Jitsu, Gracie Jiu-Jitsu or the new term Brazilian Jiu-Jitsu. Therefore at the time, the Gracie Jiu-Jitsu Academy in Torrance differentiated itself apart by its teaching methods and curriculums that taught: Self-Defense, Combatives and Sport Jiu Jitsu.

As time moved forward, the mass majority of BJJ academies around the world focused their curriculums on sport jiu-jitsu aspects of Jiu Jitsu from Brazil all a while the Gracie Jiu-Jitsu of Torrance continued to focus on Self-Defense, Combatives and some sport jiu-jitsu aspects of the curriculum, teaching and training methodologies. Today it is very common to walk into 10 BJJ academies and see blue or purple belt students that have never learned how to use Jiu Jitsu from Brazil for street defenses and attacks against punches. In addition, even though an academy's business name on the building has the Gracie surname it does not guarantee that the school focuses on self-defense and combatives in the academy's curriculum. Each lesson is mostly structured with a warm-up, instructional period and open mat session that is sports-specific year-after-year.

We arrive today with Gracie Jiu-Jitsu x Brazilian Jiu-Jitsu. There is no difference between Gracie Jiu-Jitsu and Brazilian Jiu-Jitsu in the calling or naming of the style. The differences are in the presentations, principles and philosophies of the instruction for Jiu Jitsu from Brazil. The differences are also in the academy's curriculum and training focuses. Expressing that the Armlocks and Chokes of Gracie Jiu-Jitsu and Brazilian Jiu-Jitsu are the same is a very limited and simple answer or expression because over time Jiu Jitsu in its many forms is not only about techniques. It is much more than that. Knowledgable black belts with tested experience can walk into the Gracie Jiu Jitsu Academy in Torrance, California and question the curriculum's core techniques just as easily as they can walk into the top sport Jiu Jitsu BJJ academy to question its curriculum. Single techniques will continue to be improved and for those professors that are reading this: Please look at each of your core curriculum techniques and make them better. Yet, the thoughts now are to think of Grand Master Helio Gracie's examples.

We come to the conclusions as Grand Master Helio Gracie modeled. There are good and bad teachers. There are training environments that teach self-defense and there are not. Some schools have both environments. And as we gain a wider view of Jiu Jitsu from years of experience, all drills, katas, assessments, challenges and refinements have their place, time and purpose as Jiu Jitsu and individuals evolve and learn. Our time and place finds us all failing much more than we succeed. Yet as we learn further, how we view setback, failure, tapping out, winning, gold medals and success changes too with Jiu Jitsu practice. The value of the real lessons found in the academy show us how we can find empowerment starting at the point where limitations end. Ask yourself if you could escape the mount position during your first Jiu Jitsu lesson? Your limitation was shown at the beginning of the lesson.

Why Use The Gi

Why do I have to wear the Gi? I am asked why wear the kimono (GI Uniform) to learn Jiu Jitsu as an instructor. Many times this is an issue in the Jiu Jitsu community of GI VS NO-GI.
However, when a layman asks you about the Jiu Jitsu uniform, it is important to express simple reasons for its use. You will find that many reasons on the list below make perfect sense. Share some of them with your friends and students next time you are asked, "Why Do You Train In The GI?"

1. Hygiene- Jiu Jitsu can be very sweaty. The mats for training also get wet quickly. By using the Jiu Jitsu uniform, personal body sweat is trapped inside the kimono and not shared with the mat or your training partner.

2. Slow Down- Since you are in the gi, your arms will be less sweaty and when you are in a bad position such as an armlock submission, it will be very difficult to pull your arm out of the position. Thus from the beginning, the kimono will force you to learn proper technique to counter positions. Without the gi on, the training and positions are faster. This is not a bad thing. With the kimono on, the training and positions can be much slower. This also is not a bad thing, but in this context helpful for the learning process. The best students of Martial Arts can have different speeds for performance. And as they say, "If you can do it slow, you can do it fast!"

3. Gripping- Having a training partner that is wearing a gi, quickly you will gain better grip strength in your hands and arms. This will be helpful in your Jiu Jitsu journey.

4. More To Do- With the gi on, you will have many ways to better control your opponent and you will have more submissions in your arsenal. Remember that the kimono can be used against you as well. Beware of the lapel chokes!

5. Push The Mind's Creativity- This next one is based on training in the gi with a training partner and finding yourself in positions you can only explore with uniform on. There is a sense of creativity and exploring the mind that goes with training in the gi that over the years helps you when taking the gi off for training. One day you will be in positions and doing things without the gi on that you could never have experienced if you did not use the uniform as a tool to help you bring your body to such a level.

6. Tradition & Evolution- Wearing the gi keeps you connected to your roots in Jiu Jitsu, your lineage, your team, your academy, your rank and the past while training in the present to influence tomorrow's success. Jiu Jitsu evolves and has tradition.

The Seminar With The Master

As I was driving to the Gracie Academy in Torrance, California in 2011, I was thinking about how thankful I was to be given the opportunity to attend this seminar. All the people that are supporting me such as covering my Jiu Jitsu classes, sending their praise to train with Rickson and everyone that played their part in getting me a spot at the sold out event. I drove thinking about how blessed I was to be living in Redondo Beach, California and how everything was two miles down the road. For years, I wanted to attend a seminar hosted by Rickson; however, topics such as not being part of his association, team politics and other circumstances played their part in me not attending. I was always so open to it.

***

When I started training Jiu Jitsu in 1995, I was

always told that Rickson Gracie's personal expression of the art was the best in the truest form. The stories that were told about how generations of the very best black belts in Brazilian Jiu Jitsu were submitted at Rickson's academy or during his last visit to Rio were told year after year during my journey to black belt. Rickson to me would always be the best. During the short drive to the academy, I also thought that tonight he would not really show new techniques and really get to the heart of how a Jiu Jitsu technique was really applied in application. Thoughts of my times with Helio Gracie, Rodrigo Mederios, Rorion Gracie, Royce Gracie, Relson Gracie and Saulo Riberio came to my mind in how a professor made me really see the easiest and most effective way to do something on the mat. Well the time was getting closer. Was this new generation of Jiu Jitsu students, even the Mixed Martial Arts students or No-Gi grapplers really getting this excited about a seminar as I was now that Rickson lives in Brazil again? I can only hope that this generation and the next continue to understand how important Rickson Gracie is to Jiu-Jisu.

***

I arrived one hour early to the seminar because I always feel a little part of home there due to my time in the instructor's training program during 98 and 99. Ryron Gracie was the first to greet me at the door and told me the seminar was in another hour. I smiled and he told me to help out with the kids' class. Off I went to go play with the

30

little ones. Rener Gracie had the full group in a circle as I bowed into the mat area. There were 30 different parents and family members being entertained by the class of 25 five to eight year olds from Kindergarten to third grade. I walked over to Rener and greeted him saying I was here to help. I took my place on the circle and noticed that one of the little ones looked familiar. It was my friend's son from 1998 in the instructor's program. Teaching my friend's son from the old instructor's certification program felt like things went full circle as it sometimes does in Jiu Jitsu. Rener taught an amazing class, and finally students started pouring in for the Rickson Gracie seminar.

***

After checking back in for the seminar, I walked back into the green room training area. At the Gracie Jiu Jitsu Academy in Torrance, this mat area is the size of two and half basketball courts. The last seminar I attended there was with Royce Gracie and he filled up half of the room which was a lot of people. After I shook everyone's hand and took my place against the wall, Rickson filled up the whole room wall to wall shoulder to shoulder. Everyone wore white kimono uniforms on a side note observation. As we stood there, the room got very quiet. Ryron made the joke if anyone wanted to teach a move for the opening act. No one made a comment. Rorion Gracie and Rickson Gracie walked onto the mat. I really can't remember if anyone clapped; I don't think anyone did. Rorion wore a

Red Belt and Rickson wore the Red & Black Belt; some call it the coral belt. Oldest son of Grand Master Helio Gracie, Master Rorion Gracie welcomed everyone to the academy and joked about how fast the seminar with Rickson sold out. Rorion went on to say it has been a very long time since the two had shared a mat together and that he was one of Rickson's favorite fans. As a Jiu Jitsu student for over 16 years, I knew I was watching a very important moment in the Gracie Family.

***

Rickson started the seminar with basic hip movements and went on to say how important the hips were in Jiu Jitsu. "A man can fight with stiff arms and legs, but with stiff hips; not really," Rickson joked a little. And from there we were off to the learning process. Rickson taught the seminar in what I would call an introduction style format where he greeted students and asked them what they would do from such and such a position. I spent over two years at the old Gracie Jiu Jitsu Academy on Saturday mornings teaching this way. It was the classic intro style approach. Rickson wanted to see what we were thinking and how we were behaving. Instead of hitting the mats and working on ground techniques, Rickson demonstrated basic Gracie Jiu Jitsu self-defense techniques. He told us that he was not going to teach new techniques just focus on the real basics. Like this was going to be easy; I knew I was going to really learn tonight.

***

The first two techniques that were explored in the Rickson Gracie seminar were finding the balance/base of the side headlock and rear choke attacks. He didn't teach the large group how to escape the positions; however, he simply asked different students from a mixture of academies and skill levels how they performed the basic escapes. From each idea from the student attendees, Rickson would find a flaw or a disconnect in the counter/position. Rickson in these two example techniques would showcase his guiding principle of finding the real connection in Jiu Jitsu positions.

***

The real connection is often said to be the invisible Jiu Jitsu that you don't see, but only can feel. It is the difference between practicing a technique and having the teacher say, "Do you understand verses did you feel that," to the student. The student that understands may not have the better experience compared to the student that felt the connection. Rickson used the self-defense techniques to challenge our understandings of where and how to find the connection between oneself and the opponent. The relationship in grappling is a real connection of give & take. If the connection is being felt, a student will find the leverage points in the position and be able to work more effectively with technique verses using strength and useless force. During these two techniques, I enjoyed looking around at all the different black belts practicing Jiu Jitsu 101 techniques with a different set of eyes now that Rickson was teaching. Master Rorion Gracie when I looked back behind me grabbed his son Ryron and was practices these techniques. My observation was that they and the rest of us were looking to practice the connection and play with the leverage points.

***

The next two techniques that were challenged were the basic lapel grab and bearhug clinch. Rickson asked a black belt to counter this lapel grab. He pulled the student off balance left and right. Maybe the student was nervous or didn't understand what had been asked, yet regardless of what was happening in the short discussion between Rickson and this black belt attendee we all were listening with a new set of ears. Rickson went on to showcase how to find better base with this simple lapel grab. In short, he improved our basic understanding of the skills sets found in Judo. One quote by Rickson that stood out to me during this technique was, "It is more than just the grip...I'm talking about the connection that is invisible!"

***

The clinch bearhug was next to counter. What's a basic self-defense technique to counter? Rickson asked for any experienced students to escape his bearhug. Two black belts stepped forward and did the basic Gracie Jiu Jitsu self-defense variations to escape the under the arms bearhug hold: both counters were very close. Rickson found the flaws. We all saw that both students didn't escape either. Gracie would go on to find the connection and help us feel where the real leverage points were located compared to only using base and leverage tricks! It was at this point in the seminar where many of us were starting to catch on. Younger nephews of Rickson would start asking questions about distance changes within the position while Gracies questioned the importance of using disconnection; Rickson answered with complete truth and with a certain speed in his responses. A disconnection in the context favored striking arts; staying connected was Jiu Jitsu.

***

Rickson continued his instruction standing and hit the mat with us after a period of time. We were all warm from practicing the techniques and strategies. I was not sweating too much during the seminar. Rickson, however, was pouring sweat the whole time. He was modeling excellence in his teaching approach. Nonetheless, without giving too much away in explaining the mat techniques Rickson explored with us, I would like to relay that he continued to showcase that even the high level black belts were missing the real connection when escaping the cross side position and performing the basic armlock from the guard.

***

Back in 2000, I was a purple belt under Relson Gracie and drove from Philadelphia, Pennsylvania to Ohio to take a seminar with Saulo Riberio. Saulo put us in the same position and said, "Here is my arm, how do you do the armlock?" He found the technical mistakes in how we were doing the armlock. Rickson on the other hand used black belts to show that we did not understand how to control the middle position from our guard. One student after the other performed some sweet and fast armlocks on Rickson, and each time he would show that there were ways for him to control the hips and/or stack the position to counter. Javi, an experienced black belt, MMA Fighter and No-Gi Grappler, put a fast armlock on Rickson, but there was a moment where the position could be countered. By the time, Rickson asked me to put an armlock on him, I was thinking armlock…what's an armlock…? I was thinking about what Saulo did years before and what simple armlock variation was left to do. I put Rickson in the armlock and off balanced him first; Rickson recovered and stacked me: With his head nod and a smile, I didn't showcase what he was looking for. Although it felt cool to off balance him even if it was a demo!

***

Rickson asked Javi to go into his guard. Rickson

performed the armlock and controlled the middle position. Javi said clearly that his arm was trapped and already straight: Rickson said, "Aha!" Javi couldn't stack to counter or pull his arm out of the position. Rickson pulled the black belts that helped with the demo aside to perform the armlock on him. This was my only chance during the seminar to have any golden time with Rickson. He helped me perform the armlock from the guard. And after a couple of tries, Rickson asked me if I felt the difference between what I was doing compared to this strategy. I said yes with a smile. He then said to me, "Enjoy it and control the middle!" Rickson told the group that it was very important to practice the armlock this way to put the smaller person in position to win again the larger one: One attempt and one submission to end the fight. The words echoed of Japanese Karate, and that was a saying I heard in 1993.

***

The seminar ran 3 hours in length. Rickson had his own teaching personality naturally, but I saw many moments of this brothers' style of teaching and personality too. Maybe it came from Grand Master Helio Gracie. We were all lined up as Rorion asked the important question to his brother, "When are you coming back!" Rickson joked about his new lifestyle now of surfing in Brazil, healthy living and TEACHING JIU JITSU. He let us know that his goal is to come back because tonight was only 3% of his Jiu Jitsu, yet he hoped it was 3% that made an impact in everything wepracticed. Rickson said he would come back to teach 10%, 50% and 100% of his Jiu Jitsu. And it was at that moment, he got choked-up. I understood why it was emotional at that moment for him. I was so happy for him to be there.

***

Rickson expressed that he was very proud of Rorion and the boys for what they had done with the business and the Gracie Academy, and how coming to the academy was like coming home! He concluded with the path he took of challenging himself to fight anyone throughout the years in open divisions, fighting in the ring and finding the energy/connection/ during the struggle. In all competitions and efforts, it led back to a better understanding of self-defense and Jiu Jitsu. And now his goal was to teach what he had learned.

The Meeting

By the time my email was sent to Rickson Gracie, I had already spent over a year's time working on a Jiu Jitsu federation that I wanted to see materialize. I had filed trademarks with the United States for the World Brazilian Jiu-Jitsu Federation and later the Unified Brazilian Jiu-Jitsu Federation. The latter would become my business name in California.

My goal was to see a real federation of Jiu Jitsu that was education, sport competition and community. Up until the creation of the Jiu Jitsu Global Federation there was no federation of Brazilian Jiu Jitsu that did this. The only focus of a federation such as the International Brazilian Jiu Jitsu Federation was to promote the sport. My thinking was that Jiu Jitsu was bigger than that and there were a whole lot of people that were doing Jiu Jitsu training everyday that would never do a sport competition.

***

In the Jiu Jitsu community, there was an event called Metamoris II. The main event had Rickson's son Kron Gracie fighting in it. Rickson had traveled from Brazil to see this match, so I knew he was in town. Just weeks before I was contacting respected Black Belts in the Jiu Jitsu world to listen to my idea about forming a new federation of Jiu Jitsu that was different. I was putting together my council members if you will. One person I wanted on the board was an old time Vale Tudo (Anything Goes) fighter from Brazil that just happened to be a Rickson Gracie Black Belt. His name was Jorge Pereira.

What I wanted was for Pereira to be the director of Vale Tudo of the World Brazilian Jiu Jitsu Federation. What I was thinking was the community needed a big history lesson in how to use Jiu Jitsu from Brazil in the streets. Through history, education and examples of fighters, I felt it was a good direction for people that were only thinking about sport Jiu Jitsu techniques and strategies.

During the Skype meeting, Jorge was very

supportive of my ideas. He said first he wanted to speak with his Master Rickson before moving forward. And then he said something that took the energy out of me. Jorge said, "I want to talk to Rickson because he wants to start a federation." I remember getting off the skype call and then walking around my place thinking if Rickson does anything it would get attention. At the time, I took the information and put it to the side to wait for Jorge's response. A few weeks went by and he told me he was on board for the new federation.

For what seemed to be a month for Jorge to respond, I had gotten word from the US trademark office that I could not use the words: World Brazilian Jiu Jitsu Federation or my logo because World Brazilian Jiu Jitsu Association had on file a low level trademark already named supplemental trademark. The office said I could try to contact the person and have an agreement signed. I also picked at the evaluator's brain on the phone call by asking what was available. She said try something like, "Global Federation or Unified etc." Still on the phone call she said, "Anthony I am not your lawyer and the call today was to tell you to change the name!" The time was 6:45 A.M. It was not the information I wanted to hear; however, by the end of the day I had the name Unified Brazilian Jiu Jitsu Federation (UBJJF) filed and started working on the new revised logo. In the next two months from that point, the Metamoris 2 event was happening.

The Metamoris event took place on a Saturday in Los Angeles. During the event in which Kron Gracie was the last match of the night, I did see Master Rickson Gracie. He had traveled from Brazil to see his son. I knew he was in town. The next day I posted on my social media website Facebook wall: I want to talk to Rickson. A little bit later in the day I received a message for Julio "Foca" Fernandez who was an old surfing friend of Rickson and one of my Jiu Jitsu professors. Foca gave me Rickson's private email and said to tell him I said hi.

Writing the email to Rickson for that first time I knew I had to get his attention and be meaningful. I kept it short by telling him I was a black belt in Jiu Jitsu, trained with his family, wanted 5 minutes of his time and that I had an idea for a federation, but wanted to look him in the eyes to express it. I thought that was very Samurai to write something like that. The next day I woke to receive a short email that told me to meet him in Santa Monica on a Tuesday as he was going back to Rio de Janeiro on Wednesday.

Tuesday arrived on a sunny California day. I was nervous to meet Rickson Gracie at his place. Standing in the hallway of the building waiting for him to come down in the elevator, my hands were shaking and a little wet. I remember wiping my hands on my jeans. Rickson welcomed me with a hug and asked if I wanted to talk inside or outside. I chose to be outside near the pool. As we walked I made small talk to congratulate his son Kron on his victory and also to tell him Foca said hello as it was him that gave me the email. Rickson smiled and said that Foca was his old surf partner in Rio.

We sat down and I asked how much time I had to speak with him. Rickson told me sharply that I had five minutes. I quickly took it as a challenge to open my heart and tell a little bit about my passion for Jiu Jitsu and moved to question him about the current Jiu Jitsu federations around the world. Our five minutes lead to one hour that afternoon. When we walked in the building, Rickson ask me why I wanted to do all this and start a real federation? I said I am doing this for my father whom was ill, my future family and of course Jiu Jitsu.

When the door was closing as we started to walk in the building, I held it open. I said to Rickson that I knew his secret about wanting to start a federation because Jorge Pereira had told me. I felt I had shown Rickson all my cards at that moment. Next, I asked to know the steps from here and knew he had to think about our meeting. Rickson said that I could have a Skype meeting with his personal friend and partner Carlos Gama.

At that moment, I stepped forward in front of Rickson and said, "We can always Skype: I want to meet him." Rickson looked at me and said, "Tony I can feel your heart. Carlos is in Brazil. We can all meet in August." The next day I woke to a new email that was short. I was tired from the night before from writing through the night.

The feeling I had was like my eyes were open but felt closed behind them and also dry. I read the email from Rickson in front of the mirror. It said that we have the same mission and that he believed that I was doing all this for the right reasons. My eyes begin to tear and I was no longer tired. All I had was motivation to head to Brazil.

Brazil the 9th Time Around

The goal of my trip to Brazil was to meet with Rickson Gracie and Carlos Gama to discuss Jiu Jitsu Federation plans. This meeting was scheduled towards the end-of-the-week: as I was to arrive early to visit my friends Dennis Asche of Connection Rio and Claudia Gadelha of Nova União & the Ultimate Fighting Championship.

Rio de Janeiro, Brazil is my favorite place in the

world to visit and train Jiu Jitsu. At the time of this writing, I have been there 10 times and have a very basic understanding of the language. I have some of the best stories in my life that happened in Brazil; however, the night before my meeting with Rickson and Carlos was one I never forgot. The night was the second time climbing the famous mountain in Rio called: Pedra da Gavea!

In 2001, I climbed Pedra da Gavea with World Jiu Jitsu Champions Saulo and Xande Ribeiro. During the ascent, we saw many different famous Jiu Jitsu competitors from different teams all preparing for the World Championship the following week. Climbing this mountain is simply what a Jiu Jitsu fighter does I learned. Now many years later, I wanted to do this again with my friend Claudia. The night before we met up at the Brazilian Shooto Mixed Martial Arts event. I told her tomorrow we are climbing the mountain. I wanted to do this for 3 reasons. Firstly, I wanted to do this for my father who had recently passed away at the time. Secondly, I thought it would be good luck and give me power for the meeting with Rickson and Carlos. Thirdly, Claudia nicknamed, "Claudinha," (Little Claudia) had never climbed the mountain.

The next day Claudia arrived around 3PM in the afternoon. I was nervous from the start because by the time we started up the hill; we both knew it would be dark by the time we got to the top. Even with full energy it was going take about 3 hours to arrive at the very top. The thing that we needed to think about was conquering Pedra da Gavea in the dark. In 2013, the city of Rio was preparing for many social events such as the World Cup and the Olympics. One byproduct of all this construction in the city was how the Police and Military brought more organization and safety to the favelas (slums). As a result of stopping crime and arresting the drug dealers in the slums, many of the teenagers looked for other ways to make money. The new hustle was to rob and steal from tourists and other locals climbing Pedra da Gavea at night.

At the base and entrance of the mountain was a local security guard and stand. In Portuguese, I knew the guard was saying to Claudia that it was not safe to start now because it would be dark and the bandits could rob us. I said in English, "Tell him I have done this before and we will be quick!" Claudia told the guard and he let us pass; however, he said that we were on our own with no protection.

Climbing Pedra da Gavea is a little bit of rock climbing without safety ropes, walking in the forest trying not to slip on wet roots from trees, being in the mud and deep inclines with beautiful views of Brazil. For someone that does not do these types of things, there are many challenges in climbing the mountain. It takes about 2 hours and 30 minutes to get to the top. One has to bring water as well. At the top even the hardcore Mixed Martial Arts fighters will be tired.

As Claudia and I started up the path, we talked about many things and kept finding ourselves stopped for one reason or the other having to wait. We stopped to take pictures, we stopped to socialize with people, we waited for our turn to climb the important rock points that need total focus and at the top we got lost coming down. At the rocks, all of the people coming down from the top said for us to hurry because it was going to be dark. We both remembered this group of people because they were worried about us.

We both moved fast from that point making it to the final rock where we could sit and take in the sunset. Claudia and I were both tired. I was ahead of her and need to stand on a small rock as a foot hole to jump up on the final rock and pull myself up. After I made it to the top, I was going to help Claudia up with my hands. This final stage is where the famous American Mixed Martial Art fighter Kenny Florian fell before his professional career and almost died. Years later he credits this accident as a reason for his back problems and early retirement from the sport.

There I was at the top with my one foot in the only place to support me. My second leg and foot were starting to climb the rock without any protection of safety equipment. My hands were reaching for some type of grip or opening to hold in the rock; however, the last rock was mostly flat and I was not tall enough to see what was a head of me. Ten years earlier, it was Saulo Ribeiro that pulled me up and it was so easy. The only thing I could do was make the jump and muscle up with my arms to the top. With a sense of strong commitment I jumped with confidence, my arms started to pull my body weight up and just at that moment I started to slide backwards. Before I could yell, "Catch me" and right when I thought to say it, I felt a very strong hand stop me.

It was Claudia with her one hand that supported me and even pushed me up where I was able to climb to the top of the last rock. From there I reached down and pulled her up to the top. I was tired. We were both tired and felt the sense of conquering the mountain. I just looked at her with a type of look that she saved my life. She knew it and later in the night I materialized the words of what she did and the deep thanks.

As we started down the mountain, we needed to use her watch that had a little light to guide our way. We joked about getting lost at the very top and not finding the path. It has become an on going joked because in the years that we would see each other, some how and some way, we keep getting lost at airports, hotels, parking lots and on the streets. Nonetheless, every little thing that stopped us started to give us a sense to move faster as it was getting dark in the jungle. My little camera was of no use as the batteries were dead. We eventually made it to this little opening and I did not like it as I thought it was a goodplace for bandit to rob us. Just then we stopped by the bushes that were moving as if someone was hiding. Both of us stepped back and watched the bushes move wildly again.

I said to Claudia that I thought it was a person. We waited to see want was going to happen. We were in the jungle in the dark and it was starting to get scary. Claudia said something in Portuguese to the effect of, "Look man, what do you want? Take whatever you want from us." There was not an answer to the question. It turns out that if was a big animal the size of a 30 pound rat.

Luckily this 7-minute wait time gave us the chance to meet up with three mountain climbers coming down. These three Brazilian guys had all the equipment and most importantly they had lighting on top of their helmets. Claudia and I just laughed because of the animal in the bushes and smiled without saying a word because finally we could see in the dark.

We quickly formed a new group all together. And two guys were in the front leading the way. Claudia was third in position and I was behind her and the last guy was behind me with the light. We all kept this structure so we could see 3 to 5 feet ahead of us. Now that I could see, I made small talk in English with the guy behind me as everyone stepped downward over rocks, roots and ducked under branches. We were all tired and hungry. It must have been 7PM. I told the Brazilian guy behind me that I was from California and that I wanted to climb the mountain the other day but the security guards said it was dangerous to do because of the kids from the Favelas with guns. And just when I finished saying that I heard the guys with the light say words in Portuguese. Next the lights were all extinguisted and no one was talking. I asked to the guy behind me, "What is going on?" He said, "Down there are the bandits and we need to be silent." We all got closer together so we could talk without making a noise and make a plan of action. Claudia was told in Portuguese to put her car keys on her belt loop so if we were robbed we could just throw our bags on the ground fast to escape.

We waited for all the people to get robbed and for the bandits to leave the opening in the distance. We were very close to the bottom of the mountain and the car. As the bandits went in one direction, the next thing I heard was the word: "Correr!"

The lights went on and we all started running down the mountain. I was right behind Claudia watching her movements to follow her actions. She was running fast and I just kept up. The bandit started after us with the guns. At that moment I felt like an animal running for my life on the nature channel. For what seemed like a five-minute period, we all just ran and slid down the mountain. To this day, I like to think of how difficult it is to climb Pedra da Gavea in the light and then go down the mountain in the light and run as fast as you can without getting hurt. We all did this in the dark with a little light that was not very much. Plus, we had guys with guns chasing us. My eyes as I said were watching Claudia and I was worried not of myself, but thinking how I would have to carry her if she were to fall or slip.

The next thing I knew and heard was Claudia yelling in pain. She had slipped and twisted her ankle. I grabbed her under her arm on the left side and the second Brazilian guy took her arm on the right side. We all quickly moved to the finish. By that time, the security guards were gone and we saw people in their underwear. What I saw were all of people who were robbed and it turned out to be the same group of people coming down the mountain that were concerned for Claudia and I earlier in the evening.

The people had everything stolen at gunpoint. One woman was on a pay phone making a call to the police. I kept hearing in Portuguese: por sorte = Lucky. They said their cameras, clothes, money, cell phones and shoes were taken. Claudia and I thanked the guys with the lights and did not really wait around. We ran to the car and drove to get food. I took her back to my place and nursed her ankle. We were completely dirty from the mountain. I can still remember the shorts I wore that day. At any rate, we turned on the Ultimate Fighting Champion (UFC) on the television and ate our food. I found out a week later when Claudia could not train at the academy what she told her head coach at Nova União André Pederneiras. I asked, "What are you going to say?" Claudia went on and told him she hurt her ankle skateboarding. This was right around the time that the UFC World Champion Jose Aldo Claudia's teammate on Nova União hurt himself on a motorcycle in Brazil. Head coach Pederneiras made the new rule for the whole team: No more motorcycles or skateboards! The next day was my meeting with Rickson Gracie and Carlos Gama. I guess I was ready for anything.

The Santa Monica Discussions

The Brazil trip and meeting with Rickson Gracie and Carlos Gama led to some meetings in Los Angeles soon after, and, before we knew it I was meeting with Carlos and Rickson every Tuesday and Thursday in Santa Monica, California. These discussions were mostly about the new federation of Jiu Jitsu. I was put to work with many writing tasks and research as the company continued to take shape.

Many days it was Rickson and I sitting in the living room discussing Jiu Jitsu. Rickson enjoyed how objectively I could quickly return and finish my work. He also liked my passion for Jiu Jitsu and writing about it. More importantly, he trusted me and knew I could get his thoughts onto paper.

At this time, Rickson moved to the South Bay area of Los Angeles and ordered mats for his house. Now he had a full office and training room at his house. Our meetings and my personal homework transitioned to his house. This was where I started getting private Jiu Jitsu sessions because, on top of the many tasks I was doing with Rickson and Carlos; with Rickson; with Carlos; or just by myself for the developing federation, Rickson and I started working on Jiu Jitsu curriculums. I needed to learn how Rickson did the Jiu Jitsu moves; how he structured his lessons and what exactly were his teaching methods for private and group lessons in the academy.

One interesting task for me was the question asked by Rickson about the new federation belt ranking. In Jiu Jitsu from Brazil at the time of the meeting, the kid belt ranks to 15 years old were: White, Grey, Yellow, Orange and Green. At 16 years old, the teens could earn the adult belt ranks of: White to Blue Belt. At 17 years old the teenager could earn purple, at 18 brown belt and 18 and ½ Black Belt. The master ranks in the new federation were to be Red/Black Belt (coral belt) at 7th and 8th degree and finally the 9th degree Red Belt. At the time, master Rickson was an 8th degree coral belt.

Rickson asked me what does the rank or belt actually represent? I said the belt represents a level of knowledge and experience in the academy, and also that each academy is different with its own standards. Rickson moved to the point that at each rank and new belt the student needed to be tested some how for proficiency and promotion had to be more objective.

I went on to challenge the status quo to express what Rickson already knew. I noticed each academy has its own curriculums and many did not even use a curriculum at their schools to teach lessons. Ranks were earned in the academies from any combination of time on the mat, knowledge, competition results or a test. The problem was that so many instructors taught the same way their instructors taught them and promotions arrived when the instructor felt the student was ready. The ranking was subjective. Next, I said that academies and instructors should be able to teach what they want and develop curriculums. However, their lesson plans should have objectives and be linked to higher standards. "The problem Rickson is that Jiu Jitsu does not have written standards." Rickson looked at me and told me let's create the standards for the academies. I was excited and knew I was in for a long weekend. Six months later the federation would go on to write the first standards in the Jiu Jitsu from Brazil for kids and adults that were to be used as a suggestion for academies around the world. Below are texts from the adult standards of Jiu Jitsu:

> Jiu Jitsu Belt Ranking Standards | The Jiu Jitsu adult standards for rank are comprehensive and focused. The standards give instructors the ability to assess students for efficiency and improve instruction to meet class objectives based on the JJGF standards herein. The standards represent our commitment to promoting excellence in Jiu Jitsu education and instruction for every member of the JJGF. Master Rickson Gracie President, JJGF 8th degree Coral Belt

> Development of the Standards | The JJGF Standards For Rank were convened to answer the question, "What should Jiu Jitsu students know and be able to do in belt rank from white to black belt?" The JJGF standards also reflect guidance and

suggestions from members of the JJGF Master's Council and JJGF academy affiliates who attended professional development meetings. At the meetings, the JJGF leaders helped define key issues. Although the JJGF recognizes that changes in practices by academies, professors, and students will take time, the JJGF believes achieving these standards is a high priority for students. The Jiu Jitsu Standards for Rank will assist academies and clubs in establishing learning goals and objectives for Jiu Jitsu education. A sequential, developmentally appropriate curriculum should be designed and implemented to help students acquire the knowledge, skills, attitudes, and confidence needed to adopt and maintain a physically active in the culture of Jiu Jitsu and maintains a healthy lifestyle.

Highlights of the Standards | The five overarching model content standards for Jiu Jitsu white belts through black belt students are as follows: Standard 1: Students demonstrate the efficiency skills and movement patterns needed to perform a variety of Jiu Jitsu physical activities. (Personal Movement) Standard 2: Students demonstrate knowledge of movement concepts, principles, and strategies that apply to the learning and performance of Jiu Jitsu physical activities. (Details of Technique) Standard 3: Students assess and maintain a level of the Jiu Jitsu physical performance. (Assessment Challenge & Efficiency) Standard 4: Students demonstrate and utilize knowledge of psychological and sociological concepts, principles, and strategies that apply to the learning and performance of Jiu Jitsu physical activity. (Psychological).[1]

---

[1] JJGF ADULT STANDARDS FOR RANKING: White Belt Through Black Belt: pages 4-6. 2014 www.jjgf.com

The San Diego Meetings And Principle One

As the Jiu Jitsu Global Federation was developing over a year's time before the official launch, Carlos, Rickson and I took trips from Los Angeles to San Diego. On one of the trips Rickson and I took together; however, it was during all these drives we all really got to know each other. Rickson discussed so many things about Jiu Jitsu, his history, about his father and other family members. These discussions about Jiu Jitsu were before he and I started taking physical Jiu Jitsu sessions or trained together at his house, at the federation office or at his son Kron Gracie's academy in Los Angeles.

During one of the trips, Rickson said that he wanted me to learn important principles of Jiu Jitsu to help make me more confident as a man. He broke it down into two different areas: Principle 1 and Principle 2 (What Makes Invisible Force). Later we will discuss the importance of learning how to breathe and when to breathe in Jiu Jitsu, which is a special type of principle that brings everything together. Principle 1 was very direct and highlighted his father's examples of Jiu Jitsu well. Principle 2 was broken into several parts, which will be explored further in this book. Nonetheless, the most important principle in Jiu Jitsu is to be **invincible**.

Rickson stressed to me that day that to be invincible is to not be tapped out, submitted or to give up to exhaustion. You will either win or draw. This is the path of defensive confidence and is something you should first learn at the beginning and develop throughout your Jiu Jitsu journey. Helio Gracie was a great example of this because he did not have the physical size to play the top position in his fights against bigger and stronger opponents. Also, he played Jiu Jitsu up until the last week of his life well into his 90's and during that time he used his defense mastery.

It is important to point out that when a Jiu Jitsu practitioner begins to become good at offensive moves he or she will start down the path of attacking to win. Moreover, it is during this time that instructors and students neglect their defensive practice. Rickson said that you have to go to the academy and put yourself in the bad positions and challenge yourself to defend with proper timing and the principles of the art. He said that he was always confident that if the opponent had two arms and two legs, he would not be able to submit me.

Jiu Jitsu is for everyone. When we are young, we can start out in this art and quickly learn the basic positions, techniques and defenses. After a few years, we can compete in tournaments and are very competitive with each other in the academy. By thirty years of age we are different compared to practicing Jiu Jitsu in our twenties. At forty, the jiu jitsu we do is even more different in the application of the techniques from so many years ago. We forget moves and rediscover moves. We are not able to do moves, but are able to find new ways to do old things with better strategy and experience. All along the way, one path that we all can never leave or forget is the path of becoming invincible. Those steps are walked with defensive mastery through daily practice and selfless presence on the mats. One comment that Carlos Gama told

me many times was that Professor Helio Gracie
would tell him, "Put your ego in your pocket
when training Jiu Jitsu!"

The Teaching Method-
**His teaching and expression of Jiu Jitsu is just
different than his brothers.**

When I was 19 years old, I took a one-way ticket
on a plane from Philadelphia, Pennsylvania to
Los Angeles, California. I had $1000 in my
pocket and my dream of becoming a certified
Gracie Jiu Jitsu Instructor at the Gracie Jiu Jitsu
Academy in Southern California. I was accepted

in the program and told my mother I had a place to stay when I got there. The truth was I arrived in LA looking for a hotel for the night and knowing in the morning I had to stay within a five-mile radius from the academy in Torrance, CA. As luck would have it within the first 45 minutes after the airport and having all of my clothes in a big black golf bag, I was having a short conversation with a woman that would become my landlord in Redondo Beach by renting out a room for the next year. The next day I was at the Goodwill to purchase a bike for $5 dollars, and after a little fix up I was looking for a job and on my way to the academy. The instructor's program started in the next two weeks and I found a job as a busboy at a local restaurant. In total with my expenses of: 2 months rent, 1 month of Jiu Jitsu program tuition, my bike, busboy clothing and a few meals was $990.00. I still had $10 in my pocket. I decided to have a steak dinner at a place called Eat At Joe's. With the tip, the bill came out to $10. It was the best steak I ever had knowing the next day I had a job and the next week I could live my dream.

Over a two-year period before I started college, I trained at the Gracie Jiu Jitsu 6 days a week in the morning while in the instructor's program. I was exposed to the strict teaching methodologies of Grand Master Helio Gracie (One of the co-founders of Brazilian Jiu Jitsu). A lot of the teaching instruction came from Helio's oldest son Rorion Gracie. In contrast, my Jiu Jitsu instructional group-classes were taught by Royce

Gracie and Carlos "Caique" Elias. Every few months the instructor's program trainees had semi-private lessons with Helio Gracie when he was in California.

After two solid years of being in the program and a total of five years in the art, I felt I had a great education to start teaching other Jiu Jitsu classes. I learned directly from Helio Gracie and his oldest son how to do introduction classes, teach all the self-defense techniques and of course the ground techniques and strategies. Nonetheless, when I finally got on the mats alone with Master Rickson Gracie in our jeans and t-shirt, I finally asked him the question so many years later: *What is the Rickson Gracie teaching method?* For the next hour I would have my first private lesson on the mats and not in his private home office. So it began.

Rickson said, "Alright teach me a move Tony." Wow, I was nervous but confident I could present the technique like I was taught from his father. Plus, I was a black belt in Jiu Jitsu and also had a Master's Degree in Education as a schoolteacher. Rickson quickly showed me why all of this was important, but something was missing in my introduction of the move.

***

Let me expand on this lesson and how Rickson Gracie teaches Jiu Jitsu verses every other instructor I ever met. He teaches what a student needs verses what he or she wants. His teaching is not about a well-crafted sequence of moves and strategies either. One session Rickson did something for escaping the mount with a Jiu Jitsu move called the "upa." I have been blessed to have him teach me this move maybe three different times at time of this writing. He did something the other day that made me rethink my basic upa. I stopped him and said, "What did you do, what are you doing and why are you doing it this way?" And further, I asked if he teaches these last details in his seminars. He told me that he never gets the chance because people often miss the important elements at the beginning. When I do something right Rickson says, "good," as you are a black belt you should know this. When I do something wrong he totally gets physical with me to show that I am missing something or could be better.

When a person is first stoked with Jiu Jitsu, he or she says, "I am doing Jiu Jitsu in my sleep and moving my hips." When someone is first stoked about Rickson's Jiu Jitsu, he starts closing his eyes more while he is awake. He feels more and smiles. I don't think I can be more philosophical than this. But when I stop and think about it Rickson has only shown me to be more.

Let's Do Some Invisible Jiu Jitsu

Close Your Eyes and See Better-

It is easy to express that I have idolized Rickson Gracie since I started Jiu Jitsu. Further, I want to thank my professor Rodrigo Medeiros for giving me the blessing to learn from Rickson when all this started.

I have always been on a different Jiu Jitsu team than the Rickson Gracie's Jiu Jitsu Association. When I started training, it was the common practice during my generation that you did not train with other academies from different teams. Also there was no YouTube websites and information sharing like there is now. Nonetheless, in my situation, I have always believed Rickson was the man since I started in 1995 as a teenager. And I have had the good luck or the blessing to learn from a lot of Gracies and top guys over the years. I use to be mad when I saw the Rickson students wearing the t-shirts because I was not on his team and did not belong to the association.

A couple of years ago, I was finally able to do the Rickson Gracie seminar at the Gracie Academy in Torrance. I wrote about it above and tried my best to capture the experiences. Today I am 37 and not 15 years old. I am happy to have this photo, a t-shirt, the experiences of learning Jiu Jitsu and a little bit about life from Rickson. I hope you do also one day.

During my journey I have heard a lot and most of the stories about Rickson's expression of Jiu Jitsu and that it is the highest compared to anyone. I have heard generation after generation tell the war stories of the time when Rickson tapped out the whole academy, tapped out all the top black belts, world champions and the fighters of MMA that got to spar with him from another Jiu Jitsu team saying they never felt Jiu Jitsu like that before. I have heard about how Rickson can put both hands in his belt and escape the back mount against top black belts and I am here to tell you it is all true! I could not submit or let alone control Rickson from the back mount. In his guard, I could not stand or open his legs. His guard pass is like a pressure wave coming down on you and every Jiu Jitsu move I thought I knew he makes better times 10. And, if I do a move well, Rickson says, "Good!" I could go on and on with this; however, I want to make a point about execution.

I was on the side of the mat with people watching me do the elbow escape from the bottom mount with Rickson on the top. There came a point where there was a struggle and I needed to use my physical speed or strength, or use another technique to make the escape work. Rickson corrected all of this so my first movement worked. Everyone was watching me do the elbow escape, but Rickson and I knew I was now really doing the elbow escape. No one could see it because it was the magic of timing, connection and essential detail(s) = The Invisible (Invisible Power).

Further, I hope one day more people understand and start giving Rickson credit for this idea of doing your first moves very well. A lot of what I am finding in my style of Jiu Jitsu to be "successful" is that I need to perform additional counters and additional moves in a sequence because I have always been small and/or enjoyed knowing the next move in a sequence &

where positions were going during real application. Rickson continues to surprise me by always correcting my first move to the point where I do not need to do the next thing because the opponent cannot get there anymore.

From the mount performing the Americana, the opponent on the bottom can straighten the arm forcing me to know more Jiu Jitsu and perform more. This is because Rickson asked me to keep his arm bent and while I was doing it he kept straightening his arm. I went through every variation I knew one after the other because I have years of experience. It is in these moments that you understand your years of adding more and more knowledge was helpful and important but you missed something along the way. And it helps in this understanding when you get to the last variation that you know; Rickson straightens his arm and says with a smile, "Tony we have a problem." As the student I am finally back to the first day of Jiu Jitsu and don't have a clue in what to do. Rickson pulls out some efficient technique and/or strategy, and now I have the right tricks to keep his arm bent...my Americana is now a very powerful first and last attack from the mount when there is resistance.

Principles of The Art- Are You Learning The Art Or Learning Jiu Jitsu With Physicality?

Learning Jiu Jitsu over time molds the art to your personal body type and personality. Through the belt ranks, you should arrive to the black belt and put your stamp on the art. This means you have practiced Jiu Jitsu for so many years, have specific game plans, strategies and techniques that you do well. Moreover, when you train, your personal expression is presented. The question is: Are you, during this expression, using the principles found in the art or are you expressing your instructor's personal approach to Jiu Jitsu that is teaching you to rely on the use of your physicality?

The principles of Jiu Jitsu are discovered in using leverage, base, weight distribution and sensitivity. The art has always been marketed as the style where the smaller person can beat the bigger person. The truth is that anyone knowledgeable in Jiu Jitsu from Brazil has a much better chance of defending oneself: both big or small. However, the theme here is using the principles of Jiu Jitsu and not relying on physical attributes. Nonetheless, It is very hard to take your personal physicality out of the learning process or application. Yet, that is why Jiu Jitsu is also a discipline.

On the Internet, there are thousands of videos of Jiu Jitsu techniques and instructors teaching Jiu Jitsu moves. When you really look at positions and techniques, it is important to see if the moves are rooted in and based on the principles because, if they are not, you will need to have attributes you may not have. The classic example is the role model of Grand Master Helio

Gracie and how he always needed to rely on technique verses physicality. Have you been thinking like Professor Helio lately?

Using guard passing as a way to showcase the differences between learning Jiu Jitsu from an instructor based on principles of the art verses the instructor that is teaching the Jiu Jitsu by adding his or her physicality, you need to think about this comparison in other positions as well. Guard passing can be incredibly difficult or it can be incredibly easy. The ideal scenario is that when you guard pass, you can use leverage, perfect weight distribution, base and you are not using a lot of energy to reach the cross side position. Ideally, you can do the pass with the right timing; however, if the timing was not an issue in performing the technique, you can do it slow. One of the first things people do when they lack proper technique is to try to use either speed or strength or both. Jiu Jitsu when done well gives the person applying the technique the feeling of effortlessness. Misguided speed and strength is not a feeling of effortlessness. Something is missing.

One good general rule of thumb in guard passing is that each move that you make in your approach to the side control is: *Your opponent should feel the pressure and your weight, or your opponent should be trying hard to escape/recover the guard.* Using the principles in your expression to guard passing will have the opponent feeling all your weight if he or she does not react. And if they do react, the opponent will be trying to push and pull to escape out of base.

There is a sense of panic in your opponent's actions during the guard pass.

In contrast, the moment you start to pass the opponent's guard with a fast movement and a control point that you will find **after you move**, this approach or methodology is a good example that you will be relying on your physicality when the bottom person does his or her second or third counter action. The use of strength and reliance of speed without proper body weight distribution and control means you are not applying Jiu Jitsu fully based on the principles. There is a disconnection or grey area that will need to be fixed.

If your training continues on such a path, the holes in your techniques will be filled with physicality and you will wish to develop your physical attributes. Your direction and Jiu Jitsu performance will be limited from the full potential of discovering and applying the higher levels of the art. The training sessions that you will enjoy the most will most likely be found in training with students smaller than you or your same weight.

The comment of, "I do not like to train or compete in higher weight divisions will become the norm." You will also speak in terms of sportive time limits of 5 minute, 7 minute and 10 minute rounds because you will begin to measure your physical endurance on short time periods. The bad news is when you are young you will have great physical attributes; however, as you get older or start at a later age in life, you have less speed and strength. The good news is that applying the principles of Jiu Jitsu is forever timeless. Relying on the practice of the art, you will not worry about time, speed or strength today. What needs to be discovered as soon as possible is where can the principles of the art be found?

Standup Curriculum
* Self-Defense Practice- This is a training experience to learn the core principles of Jiu Jitsu.
* Standup Stance & Basic Grip Contact- Stand up practice teaches elements of base, weight distribution, leverage and sensitivity.

Core Jiu Jitsu Curriculum
* Basic Jiu Jitsu Escapes
* Basic Jiu Jitsu Submission Attacks
* Basic Jiu Jitsu Movements of Transition

Rediscover The Basics, Do Them Better & Test The Results By Keeping To The Principles.

Speed Drill Passing Verse Principle Passing

Guard Passing Drill- Based In Physicality

This drill above is a guard passing sequence that is taught in Jiu Jitsu academies around the world. The drill is to pass the guard to the knee in the belly position and quickly get your self back to the starting position and do the other side. The instructor will put 1 minute on the clock. At its essence, this guard pass is a speed pass. The bottom person during the transition can move his hip left, right or even move north. At the moment, the top person has to do more Jiu Jitsu or be faster. The conclusion is passing this way endorses physical attitudes.

***

Guard Passing Drill- Based In Principles

77

In contrast, this second drill above is a guard passing sequence that is based on principles of pressure, leverage and weight distribution. The drill is to start at the knees of the training partner. Next you can do the drill with a setup or fake as if you are going to pass the guard to one side and change to the other side. Notice the legwork, the stance and hand positioning on the top person. All of his weight is driving downward into the bottom person's legs making it almost impossible to move left, right or even north as in the first guard passing based on speed. The only thing that the person on the bottom can do is sit up and post on the top person's head or shoulder. At the moment, the top person can use this movement to continue the guard-pass without bringing his knees to the mat. Please note that during this pass, if your knees go on the mat: so does your pressure. Keep your pressure on the opponent. The conclusion is this type of passing endorses principles of Jiu Jitsu and can be applied by all people at any age around the world.

The Hardest Thing To Do- Getting Pass An Experienced Jiu Jitsu Fighter's Legs.

"You are using your arms too much," a voice echoes across the mats. The student is sparring in the Jiu Jitsu academy with a fellow black belt and passing the guard at the end of the lesson. From the yelling voice, the real lesson continues. Like a frustrated little boy wanting to do well in front of his teacher, the comment hits home in how he has continued to guard pass and get away with so much because the training partners were not as experienced as him until today. The training partner was the same size and belt rank; same weight as him, and maybe a little stronger, but a training partner that uses technique. As the training continues second to second, they roll to the end of the mat after the sweep. He looks in the direction of the voice. Master Rickson Gracie is watching the training and says, "You are not pressuring him at all and he is comfortable from the bottom." They restart again now he is on the bottom with his mind thinking about the guard pass and everything else. A little concerned now of being guard passed himself, he gets to his knees and time is called. Off to the side, he waits for Rickson to call him over for maybe a-mini-lesson on the specifics and feel of what is being expressed. This type of mini lesson is golden time and something that will always be remembered. And with a wave, a new lesson on weighted guard passing with connection begins. Now mistakes are so easily answered...

Guard passing in Jiu Jitsu is one of the most difficult things to do against a skilled opponent or training partner. There are many techniques, positions and theories; however, we all know when someone passes the guard against us with weight and technique verses speed and technique. Of course there is a mixture as some professors teach the idea that sometimes you need to be fast when you are passing the guard. In my example above the top Jiu Jitsu player was trying hard to put his training partner in a position to pass the guard with superior grips and a fast opening movement or first technique toward the goal. From this point-of-view by Rickson and in the real application what was missing was pressure against the training partner. In the top Jiu Jitsu player's first move, he tried hard and "fast" to give the bottom training partner some pressure and discomfort. From the outside, the teacher could see he was relying too much on grips (arms), focus on his balance on top and use of athleticism. The overall approach to passing the guard led the top fighter getting swept and loss of the top position.

In the Jiu Jitsu community there is a type of guard passing that redirects the legwork of the opponent and ties up the legs. It is called: Pressure Passing or Smash Passing. There are other terms related to this style and theory of passing the guard. In the evolution of the sportive techniques, Jiu Jitsu competitors like sport Jiu Jitsu World Champions Guilherme and Rafael Mendes, Andre Galvao and Rafael Lovtavo Jr. have all used the smash passing and leg redirection style effectively. The Mendes brothers have taken this further in their examples of leg-drag techniques. Therefore, the logical question to ask these competitors is, "When do you begin or at what point do you bring discomfort and pressure to the guard position your opponent?" The answers for modern sport guard passing and time-tested guard passing from the former generations will have common truths and if we listen in on the masters of today and yesterday, we will hear the same thoughts and action patterns. Here are a few:

1. Be Moving Forward.

2. Employ Weight and Connection To The Guard Pass You Are Doing.

3. As An Overall Strategy- Know What The Opponent Wants and Take It Away From Him or Her.

The Challenges For Women In Jiu Jitsu From Brazil

Brazilian Jiu Jitsu & Japanese Ju-Jitsu has always been marketed as the Martial Art for the smaller man or woman. This is true because with Brazilian Jiu Jitsu a smaller person trains with the idea that the opponent is bigger, stronger and faster. By using technique, strategy, and self-controlled-timing instead of strength, the smaller person will win positions, the little battles and force the bigger man to lose endurance; thus, making a mistake to ultimately lose the contest. This is the advantage of Brazilian Jiu Jitsu. Brazilian Jiu Jitsu is for everyone. With a little bit of Brazilian Jiu Jitsu knowledge **anyone** can be more effective in self-defense, no matter his or her body frame.

Training Brazilian Jiu Jitsu

When I started Brazilian Jiu Jitsu in 1995, Gracie Jiu Jitsu, Grappling and Submission Fighting tournaments were nonexistent on the east coast of the United States and the Philadelphia area. The only event at the time, for example, was the 2nd annual Gracie Jiu Jitsu East Coast Championships, which I competed in. Our academy, which was the first one in Pennsylvania under Steve Maxwell, Relson

Gracie's 1st American promoted Black Belt, had an average of 20 to 40 students in all classes. It was a different time, yet amazing because of Royce Gracie's success in Ultimate Fighting Championship (UFC) 1, 2, 3 and 4. Gracie Jiu Jitsu had exploded all over the world. Brazilian Jiu Jitsu, as a system of fighting, caught every other system off guard: No one knew how to fight in the clinch or on the ground.

Overnight, Martial Artists were trying to learn Brazilian Jiu Jitsu, but there was nowhere to learn in the United States if you did not live in Los Angeles, San Diego, Hawaii, Philadelphia, Pennsylvania or Red Bank, New Jersey. Training methods would also change overnight. By UFC 5, everyone was "Cross Training." Brazilian Jiu Jitsu and its training methods helped give fighters and coaches better methodologies to practice fighting techniques and strategize for the UFC, Japan Vale Tudo, or other events around the world. Self-defense training also became more effective when incorporated with BJJ.

Vale Tudo (Anything Goes) is from Brazil. Made popular from 1930-1990 by no-holds-barred very limited rules fighting contests. Rorion Gracie (Co-Founder of the UFC) modeled the 1st UFC in 1993 after Vale Tudo matches! The Gracie Family & other Jiu Jitsu fighters from Brazil were 65 years ahead of the early MMA promotions outside of Brazil in the early 1990's!

I want to make the point again because this gets lost with time and the Brazilian training strategies do not get enough credit ...Brazilian Jiu

Jitsu helped change **Training Methodologies**, before the UFC, Martial Artists were practicing Katas, Forms, Punching the air, wrestling for pins, training the perfect throw, Kicking for points or breaking boards. Vale Tudo (Anything Goes) training from Brazil helped redefine how to train more effectively for the UFC and in the Martial Arts schools. I was able to witness it firsthand.

And if you are reading this and saying, "I was real and we trained the real stuff!" Well, you were training in a cultural mixing of the martial arts and putting it together like the Jeet Kune Do (JKD) or JKD concepts-groups. The Brazilians deserved all the credit because the new Training Methodologies were a fresh start and a welcome change. Clinch work and ground fighting techniques & strategies were refined for street fighting, and the revolution came at the right time. And if you were against the movement, you missed out on tremendous growth potential as a martial artist!

When I started at Maxercise Sports & Fitness, it did not have a lot of female students. We had maybe 7 or 8 women overall. During the in-house tournaments and regional tournaments in the late 1990's, our female competitors competed against or, at best, against one female from a different BJJ team. Around 1999, our academy had gained more experience in both national and international events such as the Gracie Jiu Jitsu Nationals, The Hawaiian Internationals and The Pan Ams. We were ready for the World Championships (Campeonato Mundial) in Rio de Janeiro, Brazil. When our team arrived in Brazil for the Mundials, there was a female division. However, all of the belt levels were mixed and combined. For example, purple belt had to compete against a brown belt or a black belt. This format did not change until a few years ago.

When I was 17 there were female students on the Jiu Jitsu team that wanted to compete against the men. All of the instructors and most of the male members on the team said no way and were against this idea. At first I was also against it also because everyone else was saying no. Then I asked the girls on the team if they really wanted to do this. They told me, "Tony, we train hard physically, mentally, emotionally, and give just as much to this spiritually as the guys!" I was sold after that and went on to promote for them. I took a lot of heat from my instructors and the guys of the team. I was told in Brazil that the women do not compete against the men. I was given many reasons why this shouldn't happen. And after all the arguments, all I had to say was the girls wanted to compete and there were no women at the tournaments, *so give the women a chance to fight the guys!*

Fast-forward 18 years. The UFC, today, has a female division for professional Mixed Martial Arts. Women from Brazil will be making their way to the big show soon to dominate all the divisions in the UFC. In Jiu Jitsu academies, there are more and more special events, seminars and classes for women only. I was recently looking for a place to train Jiu Jitsu on a Tuesday night in Brazil. When I found the academy, I was told I could not join the class because it was for females only. I left with a big smile on my face! I was proud that the sport of Jiu Jitsu had evolved to include and to reach out to more women to have such specific academy.

Problems Then & Now

The problems that women faced and currently face in the Martial Art of Brazilian Jiu Jitsu is the belief that women belong in the kitchen and not on the mats. Both the Gracie family and other BJJ academies have promoted this antiquated idea. The secondary idea has been if women wanted to learn Jiu Jitsu they should only learn the self-defense techniques and that would be enough. Times have changed!

I read recently that one of the reasons women do not come to classes in Brazilian Jiu Jitsu was because the sport is too **tough** for them. The writer and instructor, Keith Owen, even mentioned that women get pregnant! I thought that both reasons and many others were narrow in scope and insensitive. Later I watched a video of this instructor explaining his thought process, mentioning he was told to be provocative stating the classic, "They say to write provocatively," for they meaning the experts. In another section in the blog post, Keith Owen (who is a friend of mine) stated that he is too busy to have a female only class or that the numbers are just not there to start one. He argued for women in Jiu Jitsu;

however, throughout the blog post there was an undertone that he was not, but really was. There was a confusing message and a difficult topic with no one single answer. And that is why Keith took a lot of heat and needed a follow up video explaining his position.

Now I want to explore my thoughts on being tough, female classes and others points related to woman. First, business is the art and science of providing uniquely attractive opportunities for other people, so why not have a female only class? Second, in Brazilian Jiu Jitsu you do not have to be tough to earn a purple belt. To be tough is subjective. This instructor stated that to reach purple belt (The 3rd Adult Belt in the System & Professional Level Ranking) a student needed to be tough and submit other people. This is just not the case. Achieving a higher ranking is a journey about always improving, not just about submitting ones opponent.

Third, everyone is different. Personally, I did not submit any of my training partners for close to a full year of Brazilian Jiu Jitsu training. I was a white belt and remember the moment I submitted my first training partner. As a blue belt, I weighed 139 lbs. and was 16 years old. Was I a tough kid...not really! I wanted to learn and earn my blue belt. Back then it was a very big deal! I loved Jiu Jitsu and wanted to learn everything about Brazilian Jiu Jitsu. I wanted to be technical. I wanted to learn all the fine details of the art. I wanted to see my friends. I did everything I could to make it to the academy to take lessons.

Forth, if you want to gain rank in Jiu Jitsu, you have to be passionate about reaching your goals. You have to showcase your techniques, strategies and perform to the best of your abilities within your academy's curriculum & standards. You should be a good person and represent your team. If you want to compete, then you should compete, but this should not be the only evaluation for higher ranking. If you are a woman and want to start a family, Jiu Jitsu will always be there when you are ready to return to the mats. And maybe eventually, your sons or daughters will train on the mats too!

Where do we go from here? Well, more and more females are reaching black belt in Brazilian Jiu Jitsu everyday around the world. There are higher-level female students and instructors that want to have female only classes in their academies. In international competitions such as the Pans and World Championships, women have full team training sessions for weeks before these events, and black belts compete against black belts. There are women only instructional camps and other special events with non-profit organizations that help bring awareness on the topic of violence against women and other causes.

What we do not need is marketing or products sold in the industry based on a woman's sex appeal. There are more and more MMA organizations that are putting out how-to or educational videos about Jiu Jitsu with women in bikinis. They are often the ring card girls shown by popular demand! Further, there are products sold in the industry that are how-to instructional-videos with women...you guessed it in outfits for the beach! The undertone is pornographic and has no place in bushido and our respected art form that changes lives! Lastly, while I am on the topic of fine lines not to cross, if you are a professor of Jiu Jitsu, you need to maintain a respectful relationship with your students. If you take advantage of your teacher/student relationships, you need to rethink your goals as a professor of the art of Jiu Jitsu! Actions of mind control, sexual abuse and/or cult like behavior have recently been highlighted out of a single Jiu Jitsu academy in Maryland, and it has been a hot topic of discussion in Internet forums, social media and academies. All of this behavior has been showcased to fail. The Jiu Jitsu community is tight and we police ourselves. This Jiu Jitsu team from Maryland and its professor did not fall because of hate; it fell at this time because it needed too! We all move forward from here including all members of our community that did wrong or were wronged. It is a new day!

Future of BJJ The Inclusion Model

What I think is needed right now is for all male practitioners and instructors to think about all members on the team. They have to put themselves in the situation I was in when I was 17 years old and think for the better good of the sport. If you see a problem that can be solved, help solve it. Problem solving is what you do in Jiu Jitsu so this should not be too hard. And if you are a woman on a team that will not advocate for you, **then you need to advocate for yourself!** And sometimes your "team" will not be in the academy or on the mats, but in the work place or in other aspects of your life.

Gracie magazine, Tatame magazine and others, we need more press in your productions. Sponsors for women in our sport: Yes, we need it. We need to have professors teach Jiu Jitsu with passion and let more students fall in love with this art from there, they will change their lives through Jiu Jitsu!

Finally, we need more time and to advocate for all people in the art as old ideas change or die out for good. The challenge that instructors will continue to face is how to apply better teaching strategies for inclusion for all types of people. Inclusion creates better learning environments and better tolerances for all students. We in the community will continue to think that our generation was tougher, more skilled in the fundamentals or the belts meant more. However, ten years from now, I am going to be part of the movement that helps make sure that this performance-based Martial Art of Brazilian Jiu Jitsu will still have the reputation that a BJJ-Black Belt means something compared to all the others. Nonetheless, I hope you read that I am fighting for so much more these days. And who knows, the little girl reading this right now will be better off tomorrow by starting Brazilian Jiu

Jitsu today!

The Pursuit Of Pure Technique & The Parallels Of Stand-up Self-Defense And Ground Technique

Sometimes you will hear professors of Jiu Jitsu and many masters stress the importance of practicing self-defense. To many students and competitors of this generation and even the generation before them, this expression from the masters translates as, "You need to know how to escape a headlock or bearhug." The student will say, "I never learned this because my academy focuses on sport Jiu Jitsu." Or it is common for the student to say, "I already learned that when I was a white belt and it was easy." If this is what has happened to you or you are thinking this way, what the masters are saying is much more than that.

Let begin with a case study Jiu Jitsu student. In the example this student is very flexible, fast, has good technique and after 2 years is known in the academy or competition that he or she has a great guard. This person has a guard that is difficult to pass; often gets sweeps and submissions. Hopefully you are thinking of a student at your academy that fits this description. There are no absolutes as to where this person's Jiu Jitsu development over the years will go. Maybe she will become good at escaping the bottom positions and even become the skillful guard-passers able to get many top positions during training in the academy with all of her peers.

As time goes on, there will always be new positions to learn and new games in the sport being developed. The students in this example will continue to progress and spend time learning the newest material to stay on the cutting edge of the sport. However, one day many years from now "WHAT-IF" this student comes across a master that shows him by physical example that by using the principles of the standup self-defense found in the basic curriculum (a.k.a. the moves that the student long ago said were easy to learn), he would have the tools and the core strategies to improve everything that he has learned to this point in the Jiu Jitsu journey? To the expert mindset, this is not possible, and again, if this is what you are thinking, you need to know that the masters are saying and are doing much more than you think.

The rear bear hug escape technique in the basic Jiu Jitsu from Brazil curriculum that has the attacker holding you over both arms, for example, has principles that are directly the same as successfully escaping cross side when you are being pinned by a skilled black belt in Jiu Jitsu on the ground. You may be thinking that you know how do the rear bear hug escape and that is easy to do; however, we all know that escaping the cross side on the bottom is harder and much more difficult.

The challenge now is to be able to stay calm and perform well against a bigger and stronger person that either gets you in a rear bear hug over the arm and/or having the same success if you are on the bottom position in a ground fight. The question is how? If someone grips you in a bear hug from behind you, what is the very FIRST thing you should do? Now you can hear your instructor's words in your head: "Get Base!"

The very interesting thing about the stand up techniques in Jiu Jitsu from Brazil is that all of the techniques have elements and principles that are constant. They are elements of **Base** (Personal Balance), **Leverage, Weight Distribution, & Connection** (The Feel). Circling back to the example at hand, you know that the first objective to complete throughout your bear hug escape techniques is to have your personal base. Your instructor never taught you that the first thing you needed to do was go crazy, pushing and grabbing the attacker to escape with strength and personal physical attributes such as speed, athleticism or endurance. If all of these negative things were not to be applied in the rear bearhug application, why would you continue to do these things when you are in the bottom cross side position? Now I hope you are starting to understand a little bit more about what the masters have been saying all along.

The first thought that should be running through your mind if you are caught on the bottom cross side with your back flat to the ground is to find your base. And to do this first is everything because when you find the right base first on the ground, your escape methodology will have a strong foundation for leverage. In your standing base without anyone holding you and standing on the mat solo, to be in base is to be balanced, shooting your feet out, lowering your head level and hanging your hands between your legs near the knees; not higher and not lower, but here between your legs next to your knees. From here you will look like a monkey or an ape hanging your arms. From this point if done correctly, you can have a standing base or even a moving base forward and backward. As you get better you will not need your hands and arms between your legs so you can use them for the Jiu Jitsu techniques. To have a real standing base is to have the upper hand against an attacker. There is sense of power to be heavy and centering your whole body. The rear bear hug technique will be easier to perform if you add the details to make the escape work effectively when someone holds you. However, the sense of power, leverage and weight you have from finding your standing base is the same concept you need to do from the bottom cross side on the ground.

The common cross side pins in Jiu Jitsu are having the top person's elbow over the head and tight next to the bottom person's neck/ shoulder. The other common cross side positional pin is for the top person to have his arm under the bottom person's head and neck (A Cross Face). In both positional variations, the basic idea to escape is to create space and get to the guard position or create space to get to the knees thus get out of the position. It is rare but not uncommon to grab the top person to roll them as an escape. Yet, there are many ways to position your hands and techniques to use that have variations on how to escape based on how you are being held down by the attacker in the top position.

However, the game now is to find your base and from there create space by using leverage, which takes away the opponent's weight distribution. This "taking away" starting from your ground-base and understanding the feel of the position is the connection.

As Master Rickson Gracie says, *"Connection in Jiu Jitsu is mostly everything!"* He says this **mostly** because his theory of invisible power & connection also stresses the importance in the Jiu Jitsu principles of base, leverage and weight distribution. The subtleties of better and pure technique in Jiu Jitsu are knowing when and how to use these principles.

By using leverage, base and connection you can apply technique that takes away the top weight pressure inch-by-inch. Often during this game of taking the position from the top person, he or she will sacrifice the top positional control to stay on the top, and it is in this type of moment where openings are big and your execution is important to deliver. From the top person to recover what is being taken away, means he or she is losing or moving in a direction that is stepping backward in the superior hierarchy of positional dominance.

The next time you hear that it is important to practice and learn standup self-defense skills in Jiu Jitsu, think about how you can use better base, leverage, weight distribution and connection in these moves. And from there, go to the mat and perform the same principles in the basic ground techniques. Remember that the masters that say to know the self-defense skills are still learning as well and moving towards the practice of pure technique. What really can be better as the student when you can no longer do things done at the beginning because of the loss of physical attitudes and the gifts of youth? The pursuit of pure technique is echoed in the principles that are timeless.

Questioning Your Jiu Jitsu

During a group lesson, I often say, "This is your class: Do you have any questions?" My lesson plan reads, "In this lesson, the students will learn A, B and C!" One major element of a very cool lesson for Jiu Jitsu from Brazil is when students ask questions about the techniques and strategies. I like to think when students begin to ask a lot of questions in context they are beginning to think like a Martial Artist!

Therefore, the Jiu Jitsu instructor loves questions as they reflect where the student is in his or her overall development. Students that are white belts ask these types of questions, blue belts ask these types of questions and black belts ask these types of questions. There is no end to questions in Jiu Jitsu and there is no end toward mastery.

As a student, there must be an understanding of **"Trust Tomorrow!"** Sometimes a student of Jiu Jitsu will ask what if questions that are outside of the lesson or they are asking too many "what if" questions. Think right now of the skill in learning how to type on a keyboard. The teacher instructs on where to place your fingers on the keyboard. "Please learn the home row," you hear the teacher say. The process starts out slow with repetition and patterns of letters into words. Once in a while, a student will say, "Can't I just look at the keys and push each letter with my two point fingers?" "It is faster when I use my two fingers." The teacher goes on to tell the student to trust tomorrow and stick to the home row. By tomorrow you will be looking at the screen and your fingers will find the right keys at the right time! By the end of the week, you will pick up the speed if that is what you desire.

At times once in awhile the typing teacher will get so many questions from a student about all the buttons on the keyboard. The student asks, "What about this key and that key up there?" The teacher will say, "But we are working on the home row today. Let's work on this concept today!"

Your teachers enjoy your questions. Regardless of the answers, please begin to trust tomorrow!

What One Is Fighting For In Jiu Jitsu

Base

One of the most important forms of self-knowledge is to have an understanding and know-how to apply ones center and to have balance. Base in Jiu Jitsu is this. Standing base or grounded base, Jiu Jitsu students must always have this as a central theme in their training and applications of techniques. The Jiu Jitsu practitioner to help find proper leverage and weight distribution for being heavy at the right times against an attacker must first use the correct body alignment. All of this has to be with base. In your journey of Jiu Jitsu or in ones life, without base, your confidence and power are weak!

Above is a type of base that is taught in Jiu Jitsu academies that have a self-defense cirriculum. In the first picture, I have a higher posture (See page 106). **Please note that this posture is taught in 90% of Jiu Jitsu from Brazil schools.** Many attacks from the front, side or from the rear can be solved for self-defense in the academy when practicing throws, releases and escapes; however, with this type of base the moment the attacker resists with his hips many of the moves will not work as planned in the academy or out side of the street. In these moments if a techniques does not work as planned, the student is taught to do the next self-defense technique because the attacker is resisting. The main issue is that the student is being taught in a class to "drop-in base" that 1st photo on page 106 is ineffective verses the other type of base shown in the second photo 2 on page 107.

Notice that the person's hands are between the legs at the knees. The hands are not below the knees or above the knees. The hands are at the knees as a reference to help the learning curve of dropping in base with this type of posture. As the student gets better, he or she can use the hands to trap the arm if being choked from behind or trap the arms if being bear hugged from behind for example. This base is more effective than the classic drop-in base. Also with this type of "monkey base" the person can move forward, to the side and backward in strong base. It is called a moving base. Sadly, so many Jiu Jitsu academies that teach the Brazilian approach to handling standup aggression only teach the classic higher posture drop in base. When there is resistance this type of base is not the best and always does not work.

Defensive Confidence

If you win or you draw, you do not lose! The first 10 months of Jiu Jitsu classes as a teenager saw me never getting one submission win against my training partners. I spent that time defending myself and in bad positions. Just think of the wet clothing machine dryer and how the clothes tumble around or think of the feeling of wiping out surfing and how the wave again tumbles you around: This was me at 125 lbs training with adults every night. During this time of always being forced to use my defense, I learned about offensive moves and submission holds.

After the training sessions, I would ask my training partner how he or she did the armlock on me. As time went on, it was harder and harder for the big students in the room to catch me in submission holds. My confidence as a teenager went up so much and by the 11th month I can still remember the first submission hold I applied against a resisting opponent. Checkmate!

Defensive training and the confidence that is attached to it really is the number one principle of Jiu Jitsu. Defense is the foundation to build your self-expression in this art. Over the years you will use the development ranks of blue, purple and brown belt to chase after a strong offensive game of attack. Yet, the wiser black belt, who I hope is not only on that offensive path will show that defensive understanding in the core positions of Jiu Jitsu are so important when tired. Think of it this way. You will be put in the bad positions at the beginning and will be forced to learn defense. In time, when you are remaining in class and become better than the people around you, it will be difficult to be in the bad positions verses your classmates. You will have to force yourself to apply defense skillsets. The best thing you can do for yourself is to set aside training time to further your defensive confidence even when you are wearing a black belt. To win or draw is better than to lose. To develop that type of confidence in life is to challenge your self to be outside of your comfort zone.

Understanding Leverage

I am not a master of Jiu Jitsu. I am a black belt professor of this art. One thing that the masters will tell or show all the black belts is that we all need to understand how to apply leverage **better**! Each self-defense position, core position or basic technique in Jiu Jitsu presents us with the ability to use leverage in a better way. When we learn techniques without exploring more details and elements that can maximize the full leverage point that can be used, we fill that space with physical attributes, and this is a practice that is wrong.

It is only when a master shows a black belt he or she has missed this detail or this principle that a student will smile in the brilliance of the new found understanding in the best use of leverage in a single position of defense or attack. Over time the direction of our eyes focus on the core techniques and move to solving problems with the adjustments with leverage to overcome aggression or strength.

To help illustrate the simplicity of Jiu Jitsu from Brazil and the use of leverage, lets look at how to escape the two-handed front choke from a bigger and stronger attacker. When the attacker begins the choke, his pressure and strength are on each side of the person's neck. The weakest part of the hold is between the thumbs. The trick is to bring all of your leverage in the direction of the thumbs.

If an attacker goes after your neck with a two-handed choke, first use the classic drop-in base with your legs and also duck your chin while shrugging your shoulders upward. Next, step back in base and bend at your hip as if you are bowing until you break through the attacker's choke through the thumbs. Your head will complete the escape in a U-shape motion to the side you stepped back in base with. Once you are free of the choke, your hands can come up and clear the attacker's arms. Notice that you are in a third type of base where you are facing your attacker with your shoulder. From this point of reference, this type of base is very strong if you are pushed or pulled. It is easy to distribute your weight forward if pushed or lean your weight backwards if pulled using such a base.

Pressure

When the time to attack is presented, there is nothing better than to apply the right type of pressure against your opponent. The mounted position where you are sitting on top of your attacker's torso is a great place to practice pressure. This position is a fundamental objective in a ground fight. The mount is a superior advantage point because from here you can strike your attacker without him striking back with the optimum power. However, in the Jiu Jitsu academy over the years, I have heard by so many people the common expression of "I can't finish from the mount." Sadly, the answer to their problems are not in learning new tricks of submission holds or to be satisfied with thinking the better control is from the cross side position and not mount. The answer is learning better angles of weight distribution to make tactics of better pressure. The type of pressure that uses your whole body-weight in an attack makes your basic choke, for example, much more powerful.

This form of application in your submission attack from the mount will force an opponent to give up or give you the next option of attack. You will succeed with basic moves you learned in the first 6 months of your training; however, the Jiu Jitsu that you learned at the beginning in time will be different. Understanding principles pressure makes all things you do in this art better and more dangerous in a good way.

A Special Look At The Top Game Pressure Question:
Does your Jiu Jitsu top game have enough pressure? When we first start out in training, our training partners are new and do not have much experience. We begin to find many mistakes and rack up lots of submissions because the people we

are training with give up their arms, collars and back position. One of the best strategies and overall game plan in the ground game is to find your way to the mounted position where you are sitting on top of your opponent. This is a superior position. It is even better if the opponent turns to his or her belly. Jiu Jitsu students are instructed from their first class that this is one of the worst things you can do in a fight and you "should never give up your back to a Jiu Jitsu fighter."

As time moves on in training and students around you start to change the colors of their belts through hard work things also start to get interesting as your training partners stop making the most common mistakes as before. The training gets more challenging. I want to ask you again, "Does your Jiu Jitsu top game have enough pressure?" I ask this for the second time because it is common to see blue, purple and brown belts that are equally matched in hard training sessions to be very strategic in their Jiu Jitsu expression. These belts represent development stages and years towards the Jiu Jitsu black belt. During these years, the students learn many techniques to advance themselves; however, for whatever reason in the academy it is common to see students struggle to see who will out position each other during training.

Using the sportive competition mindset with points, these academy training sessions could factor in who was the best that day based on the most points at the end of five minutes or ten minutes.

Nonetheless, Jiu Jitsu training in the academy with partners that know how you play the game and see your moves daily is difficult. Often we have to use a lot of strategy, grips and gameness to out smart our teammates. We become better with our strategies. It is in these moments win or lose that we have to reflect if we are moving towards the submission or simply moving towards out-scoring people.

Many times with experience and time on the mat we feel all sorts of different types of training partners. There are guys and girls that just roll for fun, play defense, play strategic games for positions or even the training partners that know only one speed: Fast! If we only factor in the point-of-view of the top game, how is your side control? One example I feel in the academy a lot with tournament players are training partners that work very hard for the guard pass and when arriving to the side control, they starts to play with the lapel of my uniform to control or open up for a choke. Often in the next step it is a transition to the knee in the belly. This plays out all the time. The mindset and strategy is that the knee in the belly position will cause the right reaction for the bottom fighter to make a mistake or help the top fighter reach the mount position, which is a solid strategy as explored above.

But the feelings I experience, and you do too, is that the lapel game and knee in the belly position are not connected to the elements of real pressure on top. This is showcased in my example when the top fighter arrives in the mount position from the knee in the belly with no continued attack from the mount. He or she is just now in the mounted position. It is like the top fighter did four separate positions that were not really connected. There was a guard pass, then a side control with a little lapel playing around, knee in the belly and now the mount. Next the bottom fighter escapes to half guard. This plays out a lot and the roll continues with no submission finish. And the top person is left to think, "I was late on my timing, I should have out positioned the bottom person on the elbow escape to half guard, I should used more techniques or I will get him next time!"

A suggestion on a different type of reflection; Start asking yourself:

- **Can I have better weight distribution?**
- **How can I make my 4 basic top positions connect with real pressure?**
- **How can I have better angles in my training?**

With pressure from the top position all training partners start to struggle like the white belt days in the beginning. Even though training partners become better at giving you less mistakes compared to how it was at the start of your training, with better weight distribution and pressure from the top: *The core positions that you do gain to open original mistakes even when experienced guys and girls are performing Jiu Jitsu in a technical way.* Your pressure and attack start to equalize your training partner's toughness. Your confidence in the core positions goes up and you find submissions again. When asked about

118

strategy, you simply say, **"I am getting to the mount,"** with a smile because it is now about connected pressure and the practice of finding the submissions that are available with execution.

Reaching Limitations

In the defensive context and use of technique, there comes a time when you have exhausted your available options of base, leverage and weight distribution. The opponent has countered forcing you to use another technique. It does not matter if the person is a black belt or untrained in Jiu Jitsu, at the right moment you need to know that next position or discover it for the first time. Without knowing your limitations, there is a good chance you will lose everything you worked for in your training session. Every little thing that you worked for and struggled for will be taken away from you. I love the ability to watch or apply the art of Jiu Jitsu in the transitions of movement. Jiu Jitsu has helped me understand the feel of limits and how far I can go before I must change personal strategy, technique or position. This is rooted in the connection you can have with your training partner and/or the ground that is used as a balancing point.

Relationships With Other People

Since I began training Jiu Jitsu from Brazil, the Brazilian style of Jiu Jitsu has spread all over the world. Today with the use of the Internet, you can find Jiu Jitsu academies in every country and every State in the United States for example. I no longer have to open an atlas to put my finger on one of ten places in America that teaches Brazilian style Jiu Jitsu. With the growth of the art, I have been able to meet so many people. Jiu Jitsu has given me great independence, friendship and strength over the years. It has allowed me to live and travel in ways that would not have been possible before.

Positive Lifestyle

There is no off-season with Jiu Jitsu training. I remember just recently starting a new work schedule that had me home by 7pm in the evening. I told my friend that I had not been home at 7pm since I was 15 years old. Every night during the week had me in the academy and coming home at 9pm or 10pm. To keep this up for 21 days, or in my case, 15 years or so, it meant making daily choices to live a balanced and positive lifestyle. Even if my diet was not the cleanest over the years, the people that I chose to be around and the actions I took were based on improving myself with Jiu Jitsu and teaching it to other people. With the wrong types of lifestyle choices, people that start this practice will not last long. Jiu Jitsu and the people that excel at this, helps people see examples of positive lifestyle decisions. Martial Arts has always been marketed as a way or method to change people's lives for the better: It is the very truth.

Discovering Passion & Understanding Oneself

From my first formal class in Jiu Jitsu, I knew this was what wanted to do with my free time after school. Everyone at the academy was thinking about the same types of things I was interested in. Finally there was a place I could go were I felt I was learning something and discovering a passion for it. With Jiu Jitsu I could relate to other types of knowledge. School and subject matter started to click for me. By my senior year, my favorite class in school was Philosophy because I felt that after two years of training, I had experienced so much personal knowledge and wisdom. Everything made sense to me on the mats and I was influenced by people that wanted me to succeed. I could finally make abstract thoughts concrete in my writing and by speaking to others. I was growing and wanted more. Jiu Jitsu can do so much in helping to relate to who you are and what you want to become. This passion found in the art presents a philosophy that can be used as a tool in reaching goals, accomplishing dreams and gaining the confidence that comes in your pursuits.

The Master's Teachings, The Anti-Jiu Jitsu, Where Do We Go And The Sport vs. Self-Defense Issue?

I am asked all the time what is it like to roll with the master? I am questioned how do I, now that I am a black belt, learn what was taught? Of course, I smile and tell a story about when I first rolled with this master or that master. Next I tell these black belts that they need to go back to the beginning and discover the basics all over again with new eyes. To learn from the great masters, even if you have not shared the mats in many years and even after their death, each day you are still their student learning what they were trying to teach you in the academy. The real Jiu Jitsu pursuit empowers you and connects you to the wisdom of the past. Yet, we must avoid the anti-Jiu jitsu.

Recently, I was at a seminar with Master Pedro Sauer and he spoke about the Anti-Jiu Jitsu. This type of Jiu Jitsu is currently being taught in academies around the world that are sport-specific to help win medals at tournaments. Anti-Jiu Jitsu is about the applying of holding and stalling to avoid the match play between one competitor and his or her opponent. To stall the match will kill the clock and one Jiu Jitsu player will lose on points. Master Sauer expressed that the better Jiu Jitsu is practiced in the academy where we do not stop the roll with your training partner by using your power and strength. Sauer said, "When you are small with no power, you cannot stop the car, but you can learn to hitchhike."

We all understood what he was saying by the hitchhiking reference. Against the bigger tough fighters, using strategy and great Jiu Jitsu is to learn to make the opponent tired after each move he performs. In the meantime, your Jiu Jitsu gets tighter and tighter moving closer to the objective of finishing the fight. The opponent moves in an expression of ignorance while you move with knowledge. My analogy has always been, "We cannot control the ocean; we can learn to surf. We cannot control a person's aggression; we can learn Jiu Jitsu."

I hope all of the champions of today in ten years will be teaching the true principles of Jiu Jitsu. By doing this, these future professors will reach more people compared to only to the young and hungry Jiu Jitsu players that are seeking championship medals in their academies today. Jiu Jitsu is much bigger than a sport and beneficial to many more people through the lifestyle of jiu jitsu (arte suave) verses only the sport, only the Vale Tudo training or only the self-defense training. Instructional classes both private or in the group setting should be taught by individuals that are qualified to present the total art of Jiu Jitsu. Curriculums in the academy should help guide instructors on the mats helping those that can transfer the knowledge to students showcasing the different aspects of Jiu jitsu that are based on the principles and not mixed with physicality.

Furthermore, for years there has been the question in the Jiu Jitsu from Brazil community of whether JIu Jitsu should be focused on self-defense or sport? This is a low order question asked by the black belts and white belts that have a limited scope of the potential of Jiu Jitsu. At the core, Jiu Jitsu is a survival skillset before any person can be offensive. The sense of empowerment that all people can receive from Jiu Jitsu begins when the great professor can help a student end his or her limitation. The want verses need objective is ultimately realized on the side of discovering what the student needs and not what she wants to learn.

When we move away from the fundamental objectives of Jiu Jitsu and no longer understand combat because we believe that we are doing this for fun is to be in a bad place for ourselves or for another. Even though you may never have fought for yourself or it has not happened in a long time, today you may have to fight for someone else. My hope is that you have sided on pursuing what is more than techniques, have used this time to find empowerment and have the confidence to help a family member, loved one or stranger that is in need of your knowledge to be effective in moments of stress and panic.

Breathing In Jiu Jitsu

Below are thoughts and ideas from Master Rickson Gracie as we discussed breathing techniques during Jiu Jitsu. I was asked to simply write out his answer to the question how-to and when-to breath while training Jiu Jitsu.

Rickson:

> Breathing is natural for human beings; however, by focusing and learning how to breath it will increase your potential 40%. This can be done by combining "diaphragme-ic" breathing and also the practice connecting breathing with movements. Once you master the full potential of your lungs through diaphragme-ic moves you are able to learn how to help your endurance during training. Your motions will either be to recover or to increase power for relaxation or hyperventilation. By mastering the ability of both breathing and movement, you are going to add to your life & increase your potential.
>
> Examples of this in jiu jitsu are: Entering with the perfect breathing you are much more focused on the exhale; working the exhale you are able to recover as you move! Teach your diaphragm to be stronger so you are able to fight and recover at the same time.

Master Rickson exemplifies the principles of the Jiu Jitsu. His techniques are taught differently than any professor or master I have ever trained with. Although many of the masters that I have trained with that are coral belts or red belt, have words and techniques that *sound* the same with wisdom, when Rickson is on the mat and speaks everyone listens. His Jiu Jitsu defensive skillsets are truly something people travel the world to experience.

Rickson can feel like he is winning from an inferior position; when you feel you are in the top superior position, he makes you feel like you are losing it. And when you give a little bit to improve the position, he takes everything away from you. The master constantly is fighting for what he calls "controlling the middle." If you want Rickson flat on the bottom, you only get him on his side. If you want to push that to make him flat, he is connected to your weak points in the position, often connected to the ground making him completely solid with real leverage thus setting you off-balance in the position. Rickson has place you in a dual situation from the bottom, you force one way to control the position and you open yourself up to the opposite counter point. This cause and effect scenario was created by Rickson because you have the feeling you are losing by not controlling or influencing the middle core position. When you have this type of feel in your Jiu Jitsu, you will make others feel uneasy. The comments towards you will be on the lines of, "You feel different and I do not feel I am in control." Your personal confidence will go up. Jiu Jitsu is to feel

Rickson from the top position on the path toward execution of the finish feels like the real examples of the best leverage points, perfect weight distribution and amazing pressure. As the opponent there is the feeling of panic in your mind. He does not get tired because he is using principles while you are forced to use physical attributes. He gives you nothing and you are always tiring while all your strength to get things back that you should have already had. You feel late in your timing, and worst, you feel Rickson's tidal wave pressure where you are working hard and he is resting. With all that being expressed, even at his age now he still has physical attributes and has the x-factor of a professional high performance athlete.

When Rickson is on the bottom position playing defense or in the top position going for the finish, he is breathing. He is always calm and starting the training session with a lower resting heartbeat. Before you start the training session, you are already losing in the heart beat race toward fatigue as he expressed it once to me. With all of the above information about breathing, Rickson says the trick is never to redline like a car speedometer. Focus on the exhaling of your breathing, relaxing during movement, moments of stillness and make the other person redline first while you never do. Breathing is a key component that links all the principles explored in this book.

It is said that God has valuables in this world and it is well covered, hard to see, find or get.

Where do you find diamonds? Deep down in the ground covered and protected. Where do you find pearls? Deep down at the bottom of the ocean covered up and protected in a beautiful shell. Where do you find gold? Way down in the mine covered over with layers of rock and to get reach them you have to work hard & dig deep down to get them.

The main goal of Jiu Jitsu is to have a profound understanding of the basics of the art and to express the principles verses your physical attributes. To find this, you need to feel what is invisible and that is hidden under a resisting attacker wearing a kimono. After years of training and finding better ways you will need to return to the beginning with new eyes.

1. You need to discover how to be **invincible** which is found after years of constant training of stepping up and challenging yourself daily to so you can move outside your comfort zone.

2. You need to learn **leverage** and how to use leverage better than you have been taught so your execution on your first attack works better without using more jiu jitsu positions to solve problems and finish fights. You need to find your **base** and offset your opponent's base with precision in the standup battle and the magic found on the mat during the ground fight.

3. You need to find how to constantly discover the best angles and **weight distribution**s so you feel heavy for as long as you can in a certain position.

4. You have to learn to create more **pressure** and panic than you did before. Increased pressure in positions helps you clearly understand when you are meeting the right type of objectives in completing positions and finishing the fight verses playing games of control.

5. **Connection**. Is "almost" everything and is invisible. Connection is the feel. It is more than the technique(s). With having the right types of connection in a position, your movements are so much more effective and your timing is on: not early and not late. You will have the ability to read better the opponent's intentions. Yes, it is important to have experience and know what the person is going to do next. The thought of being one, two or three steps ahead of the opponent like a game of chess has a lot of value in your performance towards success. There will be moments when the person you are up against is just as knowledgeable as you and has better physical strength. Only with the connection you will feel what to do next to complete or counter attack your opponent's next move. This connection practice is at the heart of Jiu Jitsu and will be what separates you from the good practitioners in the academy from the great practitioners. Using connection will help you find the invisible power and the ability to feel the changes that are not even visible to your own eyes.

You now have an insight into some of my experience with Jiu Jitsu over a 20 years period.,

I'd like to conclude with Master Rickson when in 2011, when asked about "Invisible Jiu Jitsu," he replied, "Every time you struggle, you'll figure out where you're not connected and be able to develop yourself with smooth movements. It's that invisible force that you can continue to gain understanding of. That's my motivation today – to understand *Invisible Jiu-Jitsu*, what is there besides what you don't see."[2]

---

[2] www.txmma.com - Connecting Jiu-Jitsu Philosophy with Master Rickson Gracie – Callmbas, M.

A Story Of Invisible Power
A Path Towards Jiu Jitsu Principles & Execution

By

Tony Pacenski
M.A. Edu.

www.soulfight.net

Edition 2 - English

For more information about the Jiu Jitsu
Global Federation, visit www.jjgf.com.

Made in the USA
Columbia, SC
12 May 2019